Jim Yo[...]

any old eleven

with illustrations by
Geoff Missen

Hardie Grant Books

Revised edition published in 2002
by Hardie Grant Books
12 Claremont Street
South Yarra
Victoria 3141
www.hardiegrant.com.au

First published in 2001
Copyright text © Jim Young, 2001
Copyright illustrations © Geoff Missen, 2001

National Library of Australia Cataloguing-in-Publication Data:

Young, Jim.
Any Old Eleven.

ISBN 1 74064 092 6.
1. Young, Jim - Anecdotes. 2. Cricket - Victoria. I. Title.

796.35862

Cover art by Katie Missen
Design and typesetting by Dazzle M
Printed and bound in Australia by Griffin Press

Contents

Acknowledgements

This book would not have been possible without the vision and idealism of Patrick O'Connor, who brought into existence the club that became Naughton's Old Boys, perhaps not the worst team ever to take the field, but certainly down there with them.

My thanks are also due to all those who played for the club, for their contributions to the tapestry of sporting disaster, and especially to those who have over the years exchanged reminiscences of past misfortunes. As they say on pie nights, 'You know who you are.' And since this book faithfully records real names, so now does anyone else who cares to find out.

I profoundly regret my lack of foresight, all those years ago, in not insisting that the Missen family waste at least one Saturday afternoon watching how we went about our business, since they have contributed materially to the production of this book. Geoff Missen never actually saw NOBs at play, but he has certainly seen more than one of us trying to cross the road after a long lunch. The ghostly frenzy of his pen captures the hectic spirit of our endeavours better than any photograph. To Katie Missen also my thanks for the cover design. Jenny Missen and David Meagher have treated my prose with more respect than any opponent did my leg breaks—though unlike them they have insisted there be less of it. To the Star of Greece Café in Port Willunga, my congratulations for providing Jenny Missen and Terry Hayes with just the right bottle of wine to suggest the title.

Natalie once came to watch me play, and two balls later I got out to the most blindingly brilliant gully catch I have ever seen. (Remembering that the quality of the catch is often in inverse proportion to the quality of the shot.) Though the brief experience has given her a proper view of my sporting abilities, her love and encouragement have enabled this book.

Foreword

These are dark days for the game of cricket. As I write these lines, Hansie Cronje is in the dock, Salim Malik in purdah, the International Cricket Council struggling to eradicate the menace of match fixing with all the finesse and subtlety of Inspector Clouseau. For the ordinary cricketer, these developments are perplexing indeed. After all, we have been playing badly for years, and not once have we been offered a cent for it.

Jim Young's delightful memoir of his experiences as a grass-roots player gives a voice and focus to this base of the cricket pyramid. The many thousands who donate their Saturdays and Sundays to the game, for no reason other than the pleasure of the companionship and the possibility of some shared suffering, are under-represented in the game's literature (perhaps we're wary of letting our wives and girlfriends in on what we're really up to). They lend cricket a special quality. As E.V. Lucas put it in *English Leaves*: 'There is no other game at which the confirmed duffer is so persistent and undepressed.'

I can make this judgement, I think, with some authority. At the age of 34, I have been a humble—nay, very humble—park cricketer for a quarter of a century on and off. Jim's beloved Naughton's Old Boys have an everyteam quality. I have played with and met characters very like them; if you have played for any length of time, you will have, too. They belong, moreover, to an honourable tradition. Certain passages of this book call to mind the famous Allahkbarries XI of a century ago, whose captain J.M. Barrie laid down such immortal commandments as: 'Don't practice on opponent's ground before match begins. This can only give them confidence.'

From anyone who has savoured the pleasures of park cricket, this book will stir reminiscences of one's own. I feel a particular personal pang of recognition: like Jim and his pals, I favoured the front bar at Naughton's; I played for several seasons at Edinburgh Gardens, whose prettiness Jim rightly attests; I can corroborate, too, how testing of character is the task of playing in a competition where one is called upon to umpire as well.

Not so long ago, I was taking my turn at this duty in a game in which I was involved, and enjoying the summer scene: the mellow late afternoon light, the enchanting birdsong, the resonance of willow on leather. But my reverie was disturbed by a sulphurous lbw appeal from the opposing captain, a purveyor of nude dibbley-dobblies. I suspected it was plumb, but suspect was all I could do, as my mind was momentarily as blank as Alan Bond's in a witness stand. Shaking my head I stammered something about it 'doing too much'. The captain, unconvinced of the sincerity of my tribute to his trickiness, penetrated this as the excuse it was, remonstrating that I was a 'cheating c– – –'; not once, but for the balance of the day. He had my sympathy. Fortunately, for honour's sake, we lost by a suitably comfortable margin.

Some months later, in my capacities as a journalist, I was researching a story that required some expert testimony on an aspect of sporting commerce. It was recommended I consult one expert in particular, and duly made an interview appointment. Pad and tape recorder in hand, I was ushered into an office to face, yes, my chief tormentor of that day, the captain I had so grievously wronged. I conducted a curious interview, looking everywhere but at my subject, and with intense regard for my notes; had it been possible, I would have asked my questions while facing in the opposite direction. Finally, at the end of our chat, with no real reason for preserving my anonymity, I asked my interviewee if he recalled our previous encounter. Fortunately, once apprised of its circumstances, he proved generous and forgiving.

Ah, the healing power of time, I thought, and cricket's fraternal spirit. For a while anyway. I next set eyes on my new-found friend at the start of the following season, and extended my hand in greeting. 'Oh, it's you,' he replied, 'you cheating c———.'

I'll go no further, as this is Jim's story. But it does, in a sense, belong to all of us who've ever strapped on a pad (preferably with old-fashioned buckles), picked up a bat (with the maker's name unintelligible), or wondered why we play this slow, difficult, infuriating and utterly bewitching game.

Gideon Haigh
Melbourne, July 2000

Start of Play

On summer Saturdays, in public parks and school grounds all over Australia's cities, flags are arranged in a circle, coir mats are stretched over concrete pitches, and cricket matches of no importance whatsoever to anyone not actually taking part are conducted with a degree of endeavour, and frequently of venom, deserving of far more serious enterprises.

Park cricket is an Australian institution.

The term 'park cricket' does not refer to a casual hit with the kids, or to scratch matches and social games arranged *ad hoc*. Formally constituted bodies, frequently calling themselves the Something-or-Other Churches Cricket Association, organise regular schedules of matches in a number of grades—juniors of a Saturday morning, men in the afternoon. (Women's cricket might be played on adjoining grounds, but I find it hard to believe that it shares the ethos of park cricket as it was when I played.)

Park cricket belongs to the cities. In the country the local district cricket association is capable of expansion to a sufficient number of grades to embrace all willing participants. However lowly your own level, you can still count how many wicketkeepers, or how many donkey-drop off-spinners, or how many left-handed middle-order batsmen there are between you and selection for the firsts — which means playing with and against the best there are going around in wherever you come from.

In the larger population centres we are swamped by possibilities. District cricket (only one step down from the interstate level and two steps from the divinity of Test matches) stretches to four grades, beneath which comes the subdistrict, still playing on turf and therefore cricketers of account. After that, things start to shade off until you arrive at the matting level, where the overflow from the elite competitions is catered for by a proliferation of local competitions. The Protestant Churches, having swallowed the peculiarly English delusion that such a selfish game as cricket is character-forming, have been especially zealous in their efforts to keep the young men of Australia off the streets on Saturday afternoons. The fact that one consequence of the game is long hours in the pub afterwards was probably not part of the original plan.[1]

It would not be strictly true to represent park cricket as a breeding ground for players at the elite level. Any young kids showing real promise have usually been weeded out and dispatched to serious com-

---

1   When it comes to cricket competitions, the word 'Churches' always signifies 'Protestant'. It is a sign of significant social change that many of these associations, having survived for close to a century, have either folded up or been forced to drop 'Churches' from the title, adopting a purely regional name. This not only acknowledges the fact that the Churches are no longer capable of filling pews or playing fields, but also enables them to play on Sundays, just like the much rarer Catholic (YCW) competitions have always done.

petitions. As a rule, park cricketers are going nowhere, except perhaps downwards.

There can be no simple equation of one Association with another,
but each of them plays representative games against others, selection
for which is considered an accolade, so some rough rule of equiva-
lence is assumed. Though standards may vary, a common spirirt
inspires our endeavours.

The A Grade in suburban competitions, which I never attained,
must indeed demand ability of a decent order. But my years in B
Grade in one of the better Melbourne competitions convinced me
that even successful sides at that level depend almost entirely on the
skill of three or four, followed by a handful who might come off
occasionally; and that every team has at least one passenger who
bats 10 or 11, does not bowl, is nothing special in the field, but does
fulfil the function of making up the numbers. Curiously, it is not
always the case that he is a good bloke everyone likes having around.
More probably he is the most zealous protector of his spot in
the team. He is also, though far from the best, certainly the most
determined fieldsman, the one who never gives up a chase to the
boundary.

In C Grade, which I played as a boy in Sydney, there was an even
bigger bottom end, often with one keen striver so strikingly incompetent as to be in actual physical danger fielding closer than a pitch's
length from the bat. By the time you reached D Grade farce was not
far away.

The club whose history forms the substance of this book, Naughton's
Old Boys (more familiarly known as NOBs), competed in the late
seventies and through the eighties in the Northern and Combined
Churches Cricket Association, originally not even in D Grade, but at

a level known as D1, presumably on the thoughtful assumption that having to call yourself E Grade would have been too humiliating for the participants. That we rose from D1 to D and eventually to C Grade may suggest some improvement in team performance. Perhaps so, but it was more likely a result of shrinkage in the number of clubs in the Association.

Naughton's Hotel, from which we derived our name, is a well-known establishment in the graceful inner area of Melbourne known as Parkville. It is immediately across the road from Melbourne University, and there was a degree of overlap, not to say spillage, between the personnel of the University and the gentlemen of the cricket club.

We were not the only cricket team linked to Naughton's, as it was also the drinking retreat of the Royal Park Reds, a far more politically driven outfit than NOBs ever showed itself to be. Rumour had it that on one occasion the Reds had split on ideological lines, the Trotskyists inclining towards a hierarchical structure—like having a captain and a batting order—the anarchist faction seeking to do away with such instruments of authoritarian oppression. It might be thought that the anarchists would have preferred a more spontaneous mode of operation, but it seems the first reform they planned was that batting should be in alphabetical order. Apparently their ambitions rose no higher than substituting bureaucracy for tyranny—a modest advance, given the revolutionary possibilities, to say nothing of the injustice done to those with the surname Young.

When the tide seemed to be running against them, the anarchists followed the nostrums of their antagonists by seizing the means of production—to wit, the mats and the club gear. Several of the faction turned up at the home of the innocent holder of the mats; they fancied an extra pratice session, they said, so could they have the mats for a couple of hours? A certain degree of political naivety is evident here, since the notion of anarchists practising is internally contradictory, but the mats and gear were handed over notwithstanding. They then disappeared for all time. The club was compelled to forfeit a couple of games before alternative arrangements could be made, and the Reds continued without an anarchist wing.[2]

The intricacies of the dialectic were not made known to us, since there was little communication between the two sporting organisations. In a curious reversal of social roles, the Reds preferred the more exclusive privileges of the Lounge Bar whereas the NOBs were determinedly a public bar organisation. The publican, Simon Byrne, always insisted to us that we got more free jugs than they did, a compliment we returned by putting considerable quantities of money into his till.

So grateful were we for the largesse showered on us that, when he casually agreed to toss in a couple of hundred to help us buy a set of mats, we decided by unanimous vote to follow the American model of private ownership and made Simon the club owner, a position that conferred absolutely no privileges whatsoever.

Some may perceive an anomaly in the participation of a pub team in a Churches cricket competition, and it is the case that we were from time to time regarded with suspicion by the officials of the Association—suspicion we fully earned, but not for the reasons they had in mind.

I was aware, however, of our lack of theological depth and began searching the Good Book in an effort to derive inspiration for the team and uncover a model we could translate into action by our deeds

2   Dramatic though it was, internal bickering of this order showed that, in the 1980s, the Cold War had lost its sting. In the run-up to the 1956 Melbourne Olympics, the Party anticipated that being able to control the votes of various sporting organisations might be a useful lever, and a fully fledged takeover of the exceutive of the Eastern Suburban Protestant Churches Cricket Association was mounted. The resources of the Melbourne University's Political Science Department were mobilised to organise a successful Social Democrat counter-coup. Information about which churches in the bourgeois suburbs of Melbourne's east nurtured cricket teams that were front organisations for international conspiracy is not immediately available. In the Northern and Combined Churches we were blessed by the absence of ideological dogfights.

in the field. When I referred the fruits of my reading to fellow members, we paused with anxiety before the fierce commandment of the prophet Habakkuk (Chapter 2, Verse 16): 'Drink thou also, and let thy foreskin be uncovered: the cup of the Lord's right hand shall be turned unto thee, and shameful spewing shall be on thy glory.'

As far as I recall, this was not among the texts we were asked to memorise in Sunday School at Wagga Wagga Baptist in the 1950s for our spiritual edification. Though uncomfortably accurate (in some aspects at least) as a description of our usual behaviour, it seemed altogether too emphatic for a team whose general play was marked more by its diffidence.

We therefore settled on the much more benign and optimistic words from Daniel, 12, 4: 'Many shall run to and fro and knowledge shall be increased.' We were not sure of the educative value of our activities, but the to and fro part served as an appropriate motto for the way we conducted the game.

From time to time other pub teams appeared briefly, and the chapter on our relations with the representatives of the Royal Oak shows why those charged with the duty of administering a fair and decent competition were right to be nervous. But such was not our demeanour. Far from being a mob of louts who brought disrepute to the game and the Association, we played with exemplary fairness (most of the time) and even, we prided ourselves, instilled a degree of civility into some of the wilder clubs against whom we regularly competed. In any case, it was not unknown for the actual Church teams to be the worst cheats of the lot. I particularly recall a stalwart officer of the Salvation Army steadfastly standing his ground after the most regulation caught and bowled, compelling a reluctant umpire (one of his own team mates, of course) to give the obvious decision. It seemed for a moment he might get away with it.

In fact, in its last years before it went out of existence, few of the clubs that made up the Association were actually connected with churches of any description, and probably even fewer were conversant with the sometimes erratic fancies of the prophet Habakkuk. Such a relaxation of the rules perhaps indicates an increasing problem in sustaining the size and standard of the competition.

The President of the Association was fond of 'Warnings', and frequently warned the clubs that those without junior sides had no future. Since NOBs had only one team, and that one a distinctly ageing outfit, we were duly put on notice. All the more alarming for those of us who looked back on our past and found no consolation there for the loss of the future.

But even as he warned us, as in the President's Report of 1982–83, even greater disasters could be sniffed in the wind:

> The past season, my first as President was far more turbulent
> than expected. The departure of the General Secretary from
> the scene and the lack of applicants for the position put me
> and the other elected representatives in an awkward position.
> Fortunately we managed to struggle through . . .[3]

But not indefinitely. In the end it was the Association that gave up the ghost just before the start of the 1990–91 season, even as NOBs were saddling up for another tilt at the windmills. I suppose we could have searched at short notice for another association and a new set of opponents, but at the time it seemed easier to follow it out of existence.

The demise of the Northern and Combined may be no great loss to Australian cricket, but the instability of the clubs and the difficulty in recruiting players is a sign of the times. Over the years we played,

---

3   NCCCA Annual Report, 1982–83, page 3.

the number of games taking place across the broad stretch of Prince's Park shrank noticeably. There must have been several Associations involved, all of them hard pressed.

In the case of the NCCCA it must have seemed, at last, not to be worth the trouble and expense of keeping things going. What is more surprising is that so many people should have been prepared to devote their energies for so long in order to maintain a competition of such little importance.

There are those who would argue that sport should only ever be played at the level of amateur incompetence, but I suppose some concessions must be made to those blessed with genuine talent. And it is certain that those who put such effort into the thankless task of administering a competition like ours did do so believing in the serious value of the enterprise.

Organising such an association is a complex business, involving dozens of clubs competing in many grades, on grounds strewn over a large part of Melbourne. There are registration lists to supervise, local councils to negotiate with, umpires to organise, innumerable tedious meetings, and all the paraphernalia of liaison with other similar organisations, each impressed with a conviction of its own importance. Those who undertake such a role must draw moral consolation from the thought they are doing something for the good of the great game. At a club level we were less concerned with high-minded motives, and not much interested in achieving glowing success at our chosen (or predestined) level of competition. Our business was more to do with enjoyment, a keen sense of the ridiculous, and sharing a beer.

One might well ask what it is that makes grown men, some of them quite capable of engaging in serious pursuits of benefit to themselves, their families and their communities, squander Saturday afternoons trying to do something they will never be any good at, risking ridicule and physical injury, braving the hole in the ozone layer, or the more occasional hazard of wandering elephants, for no reward whatsoever.

There is one immediate answer to this question, which is the amount of beer it is necessary to drink afterwards. But there is no law against spending the whole afternoon in the pub without the four hours of running around beforehand, so one must seek an explanation in the spiritual benefits conferred on the participants. No game has spawned more nonsense than has cricket, congratulating itself on its uniquely uplifting qualities—none of which were to be found on the playing fields of the Northern and Combined Churches. More characteristic was an excess of aggression and a misplaced zeal for victory such as to provoke the traditional Australian call to order: 'We're not bloody well playing for sheepstations, mate.'

We at NOBs did not delude ourselves that were were enhancing the nobility of our characters. Instead we appreciated the special insight into human folly—in friend and foe alike—that competitive sport affords.

In short, this book attempts to record the deeds of a more or less honest bunch of toilers who, over a period of ten years or so, did nothing to improve the standard of Australian cricket but did their best to enjoy life without completely disgracing themselves. We did not always achieve the second of these aims, but the first was kept constantly in view.

1

In My Beginning is My End

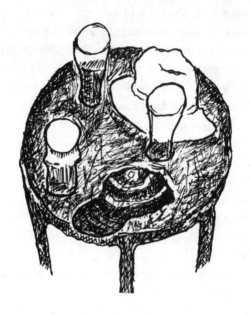

Naughton's Old Boys Cricket Club (originally named Northcote High School Old Boys) came into existence in circumstances that foreshadowed its eventual demise. It was in response to an advertisement placed by the Northern and Combined Churches Cricket Association in the *Northcote Leader*: 'Cricket teams wanted.'

Touting for teams is almost certainly a sign of an Association on the brink of extinction. Accepting a team like NOBs might well seal the issue. As things turned out, our demise was a result of the whole competition folding up. We may have scraped for players every week, but in retrospect the Association was scraping for teams every season. The death of the elephant is accompanied by the death of many ants.

I have no idea how many other teams rallied to the call back in 1978, but the advertisement did not pass unnoticed in the staff room of Northcote High School. Pat O'Connor's attention was drawn to it by one of his colleagues, who suggested they get together a team and enter. Arrangements were left to Pat, who lodged the papers and was then faced with the task of assembling an eleven to take the field.

Recruits were forthcoming: Bernie O'Brien, our inaugural captain; Clem Simonetto, beginning a long and comical career with the new ball; Byron Miller, an American baseballer who never came to terms with a ball that hit the pitch but could dispatch a full toss low over third base with frightening velocity. Sam Gerakis was another whose cultural heritage did not include the noble game. He was emphatically described by Pat as 'the worst cricketer ever to play for NOBs.' When I raised a quizzical eyebrow, Pat underlined his comment by saying, 'He was worse than me'—which seemed to seal the issue.

As the nucleus formed it became clear that the esteem in which the original proposer of the scheme was held by his colleagues was such that either he and Pat would take the field as a lonely twosome, or a rather more complete team might be collected without him. In sophisticated gentlemen's clubs a single black ball is usually enough, but here it was more like sheep shit. Thus the 'onlie begetter' never in fact played for the club, a circumstance that introduced severe complications to staffroom procedures. School staffrooms are perennially overcrowded places, and shared work areas invite demarcation disputes, but to take umbrage as far as storming off to the woodwork room, comandeering a power saw, and defining your territorial rights by sawing a desk in half suggests why the rest of the staff were reluctant to share Saturday afternoons, as well as the whole working week, with such a winsome personality.

Nevertheless, it was clear there was going to be some shortfall in the numbers, and Pat was forced to take measures which were to have severe consequences for the character of the team.

My parents always enforced upon me that the first step down the primrose path leads on inescapably to dissipation and destruction, and so it proved to be for the NOBs. Pat's first recourse was to his drinking mates, a choice which proved to be definitive in the history of the club.

It was perfectly reasonable on Pat's part to ask Max Radcliffe to play in the club's inaugural game, but it was certainly out of order for Max to turn up late and dismiss one of his new teammates from the field, on the assumption that he was the substitute filling in for Max himself.

The bewildered player, Tim Costello (not the famous one), meekly left the ground and never played again after such summary treatment.

It took a little while for a basic truth to sink in, but this was by nature a pub team, and the locus of power moved swiftly from the Northcote staffroom to the public bar of Naughton's Hotel.

There was some justification for this. One whip around the staffroom will uncover all likely recruits, whereas the public bar supplies a more fluid population, some too fluid for any kind of sporting pretence, others capable of filling the gaps bound to occur on account of accident, injury, prior engagement, apathy, downright antagonism, or simply being ordered off by Max Radcliffe. One complication at least never arose to trouble the selectors. No one in the history of the club was ever dropped for actual incompetence.

Cricket is a game that prides itself on the richness of its traditions, and this lurch from Northcote to Naughtons gave us our major connection with an enduring tradition of the game—its close affinity with alcohol.

My own demure upbringing and a few seasons with a Baptist church team had not taught me all I should have known about this essential element, but my first game in Melbourne began my education. My new team, a hard-bitten outfit called St George's, were playing Syndal Baptists and were intent on righteous revenge. In the last game of the previous season, we (well, not me, but the rest of them) had belted the living daylights out of the pious Baptists, only to be reported to the Association for 'excessive talk about alcohol on the field'. Evidently this had consisted, on a stinking hot February afternoon, of various exhortations to the bowler, as Syndal's batting fell apart, to the effect, 'Let's have another wicket and get an early start in the pub.'

We were duly fined for our indiscreet conversation and never again in the four years I played with the club did we ever beat Syndal Baptists, though I'm not convinced divine intervention was the immediate cause.

NOBs, however, was a team more-or-less organised around alcohol. The Friday evening gathering in the bar was a habit that predated the foundation of the club—it could even be said to have been the necessary pre-condition for its existence.

We thought we were just hitting the piss of a Friday night, but in the days of our lingering retirement sociologists have arisen to inform us that we were engaged unknowingly in the life-enhancing activity of male bonding. No sooner did sports psychologists appreciate the significance of this process than the Rugby League players of Australia began to give us uplifting examples—such as one session in which the captain of the national team got himself so tightly bonded that he couldn't give the taxi driver his home address. It was obliging of the cabbie to drop him off on the steps of the nearest police station — a destination NOBs tried to avoid.

It takes a great deal to embarrass a Rugby League player, but proliferating reports of what their heroes were getting up to began to alarm the governing bodies of the sport. The New South Wales Rugby League, in preparing for an interstate game against Queensland, therefore decided (mistakenly) to attempt to eliminate alcohol from the bonding process. They sent the boys off to some macho camp site in the hills and—choosing what might be called the 'Marlboro option'— put them all on horseback for a romp in the bush. Three fell off, one sustaining a broken collar bone. A non-participant in the ensuing match, he was nevertheless especially well equipped to share the disappointment of a one point loss.

NOBs seldom ventured far enough from its central city bar to encounter livestock of any kind, and our only dealings with horses were through the intermediary of bookmakers[1], so we avoided, by default, one novel method of disgracing ourselves.

Another failed experiment in avoiding the alcoholic connection was the very public vow of abstinence by the entire Victorian cricket team for the 1998–99 season. Though the pledge was loudly applauded in the press it was viewed with dubiety from our nook of the bar. Their season began with a boom and finished with a whimper, which came as no surprise to those of us much more experienced in the ways of the game than any bunch of twenty-year-olds—however talented they may be.

A slightly more tolerant approach could be discerned in a quotation I stumbled across from A.G. Steel, captain of England in the 1880s, which I circulated for discussion at one Friday night training session.

---

1   This statement does overlook the pony riders of Royal Park with whom we once came into collision (see Chapter 10).

A cricketer should live a regular life and abstain at table from all things likely to interfere with his digestion and wind. Above all else smoky rooms should be avoided. A small room, filled with ten or more men smoking as if their very existence depended on the amount of tobacco consumed, soon gets a trifle foggy, and the man who remains there for long will find next morning on wakening that his head feels much heavier than usual and his eyes are reddish and sore. A captain should never hesitate to speak to his team on these matters should he think a warning or rebuke necessary.

The necessity of moderation in drink is happily a thing few cricketers require to be reminded of. There are many opinions as to what is the best drink for men when actually playing. By best we mean that which does least harm to the eye. In hot weather something must be drunk, the question is what? Our experience is that beer and stout are both too heady and heavy, gin and ginger beer are too sticky and sweet to the palate, ouzo is all right if playing in Corfu. In our opinion, shandygaff, sherry, or claret and soda are the most thirst quenching, the lightest and the cleanest to the palate. In a long innings the heat and dust are apt to make the mouth very dry and parched and a clean drink is especially desirable.

Although long innings were not something we had written into our game plan, the governing sentiment was widely applauded. A clear majority was in favour of (a) playing in Corfu, (b) not drinking ouzo elsewhere. Shandy-gaff, sherry, and claret-and-soda were all considered from the width of the public bar and rejected. There were no calls at all for ginger beer during the team meeting. Headiness and heaviness weighed more seriously in our approach to the game. In NOBs's case, it was not so much unnecessary as completely useless to encourage moderation.

With reference to possible smoking restrictions, some of the more liberal members raised objections to the captain's disciplinary authority until the word 'tobacco' was pointed out to them. In any case 'eyes reddish and sore' seemed like a pretty accurate description of the general team turnout, so we voted against all restrictions in this particular regard.

At the level of sport where we competed—pretty close to the bottom rung—very few players (none at all, as far as I recall) joined the team as a result of seeking out a competition where they could test their skills at their chosen level. Every new member was dragooned by a mate already in the side, or just drawn into the vortex of the whirlpool by being a Naughton's drinker.

Before pubs around our cities got so deplorably tarted up, and discos and poker machines elbowed honest drinkers out of their favourite corners, every public bar across the country had its quota of ex-sportsmen, most of them very properly retired from competition at a modest level of achievement. The fact that no one you drank with had ever seen you play made it possible to talk about your favoured game with a great deal of authority and certainty.

Happy men, untroubled by progressive slogans about 'accountability'! Pat's experiment of actually putting a team on the field deprived many of us of the comfort we enjoyed in our self-appointed expertise, and exposed us to judgement on the basis of personal performance.

Having begun its existence under the name Northcote High School Old Boys before discovering its true identity, NOBs was fortunate in being able to beg favours in a useful quarter. Though we were entirely bereft of funds, the considerable resources required to put a cricket team on the field—a set of mats as well as the paraphernalia of bats, pads, stumps and so on—were made available on approach to the sportsmaster for discards from the school's sporting equipment. It is fair to say that this modest raid on Education Department resources did not deprive the youth of Victoria of anything very much worth having.

The bats we inherited were somewhere short of the highest class. They looked impressive and carried famous signatures, but the way they felt when actually used suggests that, even before the game's recent woes, top players were taking their cut for something rather less than top quality. The spring, whip and suppleness of willow were not characteristic of NOBs' play at any stage, and some were inclined to blame this on the unyielding nature of the bats we used. In truth the explanation lay a little nearer home.

As the club's kitty grew, courtesy of chook raffles in the public bar, we were able to lash out and buy some gear of our own. Our first venture in this direction was clearly a mistake, though it taught us to treat the 'Made in Pakistan' label with caution. Pat was delegated to buy a new bat, which he produced, informing everyone of its manifold virtues. Unfortunately, Pat's knowledge of batsmanship carried over into his assessment of equipment. The first player to take it out to the middle called for a replacement after two balls, and seriously thought of retiring hurt, suspecting a fractured wrist. Someone tried bouncing a ball up in the air off it, and swore it was like having your hand hit with a hammer. Thereafter it found its function as the identifying signal the square leg umpire takes out with him to distinguish himself from the fieldsmen. It wasn't even all that well suited to this purpose, since Pat had selected an item designed for the under-twelves, and someone of even moderate height could only lean on it with the upper body listing at an uncomfortable angle.

The quality of bats in the kit fluctuated, a good one being used by everyone who could get his hands on it until it ceased to be a good one, at which point we all awaited the time when club funds allowed the purchase of a replacement—a task never again entrusted to Pat.

One or two players owned their own bats—an infallible sign of having in the past competed at a serious level and now come down in the world. Very rarely, a grudging loan was made to a team mate of one of these altogether superior items of equipment—always liable to damage in the hands of an incompetent performer.

The pads we had to make do with were standard club issue in those pre-Velcro days. They all had leather straps thin enough to bite painfully into the back of the leg, pierced unevenly with holes so subtly spaced that no one who ever put them on found a comfortable fit. One notch was so tight it cut off circulation, the next so loose the pad might do a half circle around the leg before you finished the first run. You could (and often did) set off for the quick single clutching the top of the right pad to make sure it didn't get skewed so far round you couldn't bend your knee, and either fell over mid-pitch or finished the run hop-skip-and-jumping the last five yards.[2]

In our years of retirement, where we too are experts on the game, television commentary by Ian and Ritchie and Tony and all the chaps is full of remonstrations about the folly of turning blind. In our playing days, we were more worried about turning lame.

In the matter of selecting a pair of pads for the purpose of going out to bat, the range was limited. Apart from spares suitable only for sitting on on bindi-eye infested grass, there were as a rule three usable pairs of pads in the kit, one more-or-less acceptable, always seized by the more alert opening bat. Number two did what he could. Number three was given the respect Australian cricket teams always accord to the best bat in the side—but also the worst pads. Number four always knew who he hoped would get out first. From there on down it was a lottery.

2   Cricket grew up on Imperial measures, and that tradition is honoured in this book. A pitch was always 22 yards long when I played, and the very notion of 20.12 metres is quaintly absurd. Besides, if you can only throw the ball as far as I can, treating the two as interchangeable units can give you a ten percent stronger arm.

Abdominal protectors (always called 'boxes', and the subject of endless if predictable ribaldry) were supplied, but were themselves a risky proposition. The sharing of such intimate apparel invites the risk of communicable diseases, and this is an area where one is forced to trust the judgement and discretion of one's team mates—though I never knew anyone to complain that he'd caught the clap in quite this manner. The best we could do in the way of hygiene was to wash it under a tap if there was one close enough, failing that wave it in the desiccating summer air and ask, 'Who wore this one last?'

A more immediate hazard was that ours were made of cheap plastic, not always carefully filed down at the edges. Jagged plastic in such proximity to vulnerable regions can provide unpleasant experiences. Moreover, they were usually of a type that is moulded in two halves which are then fused together. Every park cricketer has heard of a perhaps mythical occasion when a batsmen was struck square on in the vitals. The central part of the protector split at the seam, though top and bottom remained intact. On impact the two halves sprang apart momentarily, just long enough for the testicles to drop through, before the box snapped shut again. True or not, the mere story is enough to bring tears to the eyes and induce a certain nervousness as one arranges oneself before taking to the crease.

We were, however, egalitarian in providing what protection we could in this vital area—unlike the English police force. On a visit to England in 1981 I stayed in the town of Halifax with Pat's brother Tim, a stalwart sergeant of the West Riding force.

Halifax has suffered from adverse publicity in recent years. Max Radcliffe's father spent an appreciable portion of WWII stranded on a troop train in Halifax, and always claimed it was the only place in England where they left the lights on hoping the Germans would bomb it. Under the Poor Laws of past centuries, the beggars of Yorkshire rated in descending order the treatment to be suffered by hapless wretches in various localities: Hull, Hell, and Halifax.

This was immediately following the riots in Toxteth and Brixton and various other localities. It was also the 600th anniversary of Wat Tyler and the Peasants' Revolt, and some of the more historically conscious graffitists of London were suggesting it was time for a full scale re-enactment. Tim was able to inform me that the hierarchy was greatly concerned about the safety of its members in the front line of crowd control.

Any available riot shields were already deployed in Belfast, and there was no standard item of issue affording full body protection. As the noble bobbies faced the hostile throng, their custom of linking arms may have given stability to the line, but also presented an attractive area of vulnerability. As an interim measure, some gentleman of the old school had come up with a very English resource for their protection—namely, cricket boxes. A mass order was duly placed (one hopes with Lilywhites of Piccadilly to give an authentic flavour to the transaction), but some functionary had carefully thought of the cost factor, and ordered two different grades. Accordingly, Men's sizes were issued to officers, and a Junior size—cheaper because smaller—to constables, who were forced to fit themselves in as best they could. It is instructive to see a class society in action.

As it happened, the precautions proved unnecessary, at least in the West Riding. The young blades of Halifax did gather with mayhem on their minds, but after an hour or so they dispersed because they couldn't think of anything to do. Sergeant O'Connor said it was the quietest night of his working life. This suggests a certain lack of excitement in the public life of Halifax. They did, however, have the Yorkshire Ripper in their midst, which was some compensation.

But to return to ground level—the mats spoken of above are the *sine qua non* of Australian park cricket, for these are matting competitions absolutely. In making this claim I pass with contempt over the modern invention of synthetic turf, a scruffy green substance glued to the concrete base. No one I know can give a convincing report of how synthetic turf shapes up after being buried under six inches of sand for the footy season and then scraped clean by a rough-and-ready bobcat driver. A more venerable tradition is the malthoid surface. A bitumen-like strip stuck to concrete promises what it delivers: a wickedly devious surface in the full heat of summer, the ball gripping and turning like an old Brisbane sticky; the casual joins of the less-than-meticulous pitch-layer providing a small but significant ridge just outside off stump from which the ball will jag back in life-threatening manner; the promise of air bubbles under the malthoid when the glue loses its virtue, so that the ball hits a bursting balloon and skids into the base of the middle stump. Nevertheless, fine cricketers have played on malthoid and who am I to disparage them? Well—I'm a matting cricketer, and I stick to what I know.

In England it seems the soil is yielding enough for any reasonably level area to be rolled a few times in order to produce some kind of pitch. The Australian sun frustrates such ambitions. Without special soil selection, plentiful water and constant rolling, the pitch becomes completely unplayable: a maze of cracks from which the ball can deviate at any angle. Twenty-two yards of concrete is cheap by comparison, and the sport is opened up to thousands who would otherwise never find a game. Park cricketers should be grateful to those back in the thirties who put enough pressure on local councils to have so many pitches implanted, and to those since who have kept them up to scratch.

Coir matting stretched over the concrete gives lively bounce from a true surface, all of which makes for a testing and entertaining way of playing the game. Those who have not played on it—by which I mean really good players, nurtured all their lives on turf—do not know what they have missed.

At the turn of the century turf wickets were apparently beyond the skill of South African groundsmen, and early Test matches there were played on the mat. The great S.F. Barnes must have been unplayable:

49 wickets in four Tests at 8.5 runs apiece. At a later period, the Australian team returning from the miserable Ashes tour of 1956 faced Fazal Mahmood at Karachi—all out for 80. Park cricketers may lack the silken skills of their Test match counterparts, but we are thoroughly accustomed to getting in under the lifting ball and helping it up and over the fine leg boundary—and even apart from that, experience has taught us to be very quick off the mark in grabbing a stump when things become a bit willing. A couple of park cricketers were clearly needed in Karachi.

Beyond the ideal of true bounce and fast carry off the mat, there are some local complications. One is knowing how zealously the broom should be wielded before the mats are laid. First day of the game, no one knows who will be batting, so it's best to make sure all pebbles are swept clear in case it is your own head that's at risk. But if you are the visiting side and due to bat the second week, it's always advisable for someone to get to the ground early enough cast an eye over the pitch before the mats go down. The judicious kicking of a few stones to somewhere around a good length can create a minefield.

The physical condition of the mats themseves is also a factor of some importance. Wear and tear takes its toll, especially at the point where the fast bowler's foot lands in the first stride after delivery, as well as the spots around the crease line, where feet shuffle and bats tap nervously. Leather patches can prolong the life of the mat, though a cheaper expedient is to turn it over so only left handers get tripped up, which is after all no more than they deserve. A variation on this is to swing the mats round, leaving holes and tatters around mid-pitch, which can be disconcerting. Mid-pitch is about where a really hopeless bowler lands every ball — or even a goodish park cricket bowler perhaps once an over. If the ball hits concrete rather than coir, an unexpectedly dead bounce results. Worse still, if it hits half-on, half-off, the result might be a mulleygrubber that hits your big toe; or a bouncer that flies past your ear; or a huge leg-cutter that gives third slip a fright on its way for four byes.

We struggled on for two seasons with less than satisfactory cast-offs from Northcote High (the parsimony with which the Education Department treats its hangers-off!), and opposing teams were justified in complaining. It was obvious that new ones would have to be bought, severely straining the club's budget.

This necessity, as it turned out, marked a new era in NOBs's development. In casual conversation with Simon Byrne, the publican at Naughton's, Max Radcliffe mentioned we were up for new mats. Simon asked, 'About how much would they cost?' Two hundred and forty dollars was the sum named, to which Simon said, 'I could throw that in for you.'

Such was our astonishment that, amid universal acclamation, we changed our name on the spot, abandoning the pretence of Northcote High School Old Boys, while preserving (even more elegantly) the acronym and becoming Naughton's Old Boys.

The mats were duly purchased and brought into the public bar for blessing, a ceremony performed by bar manager and Club Patron, Adrian Keeley, who intoned various words of sacrilegious intent and poured over them a glass of red wine, straight from the cardboard box behind the bar. We were properly launched as a pub team, and the set of mats sufficed us for the rest of the club's playing history.

In recognition of his philanthropy, Simon Byrne was formally appointed Club Owner, a post he denied if serious sportsmen entered the bar. With this step towards Americanisation we decided to go the whole hog, and scrapped the parochial award of 'Best and Fairest', replacing it with the MVP ('Most Valuable Player'). This occurred in that brief window of astonishment when TV networks got the technology to bring us gridiron and baseball and ice hockey all live and lively, before pay-for-looking took it all away again. Late night owls with a taste for sporting contests of any kind, we watched with amazement as large crowds were pumped up by video screens and Wurlitzer organs to roar and scream and chant slogans—especially when nothing was happening on the field to justify any reaction at all.

Mass hysteria in the crowd was unknown in matches where NOBs competed—the total absence of spectators being one explanation. However, the sight of large numbers of people making complete fools of themselves did strike a chord with those of us who regularly turned out for the club, and we happily surrendered ourselves to the bracing blasts of fully professional organisation.

Intent on setting up the necessary apparatus we appointed an array of officials, though few of them had any function whatsoever. We settled on Charlie Doherty, a front bar regular, as coach, so that we could sack him out of hand, since all clubs of any prestige sacked coaches regularly. Charlie's major contribution to our on-field performance was to ask every week (whether or not the match was only half over) if we'd won. On the rare occasions when the answer was yes, he would unfailingly follow up with 'What—did they take the bell out of the ball?' The hilarity of this remark was never lost on Charlie himself.

Around this time the football clubs of Melbourne were falling over each other to try to find Liberal party politicians to become their Number One Ticketholder.[3] We weren't likely to find any such crea-

---

3   When the Carlton Football Club bestowed the honour on Malcolm Fraser, Frank Anderson, member of a legendary half-back line in the 1940s, showed me his Past Player's medallion which carried the same number and saying, 'That's the only Number One ticket as far as I'm concerned.' In an attempt to emulate the more affluent clubs, South Melbourne were sufficiently distracted to appoint Bob Hawke. When they moved to Sydney he denounced their betrayal and resigned his membership. A couple of years later he purchased his harbourside mansion in the northern capital. Essendon copped Andrew Peacock and Peter Costello, which tells you all you need to know about them.

tures in the public bar at Naughton's so we leaned a little to the left and made Frank Strahan our Number One Member. As University Archivist he had an entry in *Who's Who*, which in our book qualifies as fame. Living a hundred yards or so from our ground, he would actually pause and watch us on his way to the pub on Saturday afternoons, so he was clearly the man for the job.

Frank Hannigan, despite his adamant refusal, became our Fitness Adviser. Frank devoted hours and years to assisting any number of University sporting teams and categorically denied any responsibility for such motley beerswillers as he knew us to be. It may have damaged his professional reputation, but we were making the appointments and he had no say in the matter. Anyway, he never knocked back an invitation to club dinners.

The early eighties were the years that saw the rise to public notice of sports psychologists. We saw little use for such hyper-commitment to victory, so appointed instead a Club Philosopher, Dr Barry Taylor. His beard proclaimed a depth of wisdom that was borne out by his pronouncements on the occasions he was called on for an opinion. There was some talk of appointing a second Club Philosopher, since an opinion without a disagreement scarcely qualifies as philosophy—but this came to nothing. It was clear that Barry gave us all the gravity and sagacity we could cope with.

Few of our activities as a team (apart from actually playing—which scarcely counts for much) were conducted far from the benevolent supervision of Bar Manager Adrian Keeley. His considerable girth was in proportion to his conviviality, and he was an ideal choice as Club Patron. By presenting the annual award of a bottle of prize top-shelf drinking to the MVP he gave himself the opportunity of making a speech at the annual club dinner in which the efforts of all and sundry were reduced to their proper proportions. But since he did this every Friday and Saturday night anyway no further harm was done to sensitive egos.

We early recognised the necessity that all organisations need to be 'headed up', which required us to appoint a Club President. Max rightly reminded us that presidents have to be tall, which immediately settled the issue; Clem Simonetto, undoubtedly the tallest player in the side, became President, a role he fulfilled with a dignity becoming his height. Linguistic folly led some to refer to him as 'Il Presidente'—others as 'Il Duce'. Clem wore all titles with an easy elegance and, since a regular appearance at Naughton's for Friday night training was all the post required, performed his duties as to the manner born.

One position only (later divided into two since the workload was irksome) involved actually doing anything: namely, Club Secretary. He was required to receive, and on occasions reply to, communications from the Association. He was responsible for hiring a ground from the City Council, supplying the Association with lists of registered players (on which more will be said later), ringing through the scores at close of play, and attending Association meetings. This last was a necessary duty, since there was a fine for not being represented—a heavy drain on a club as impoverished as we were.

Actually, the main business of the delegate at these meetings was to attend to all the other fines imposed on us during the course of the last month's matches—almost never for ungentlemanly behaviour, like many other clubs, but almost always for starting late, and having players improperly kitted out.

It was a feature of NOBs's turn out that if a player did not possess a regulation white jumper he would make do with something as close as possible—like Biddo's navy blue number, and the deep claret sported by Steve Carroll (who later defected to the Royal Park Reds, so I suppose the signs were always on the wall). The Club Founder himself never quite caught up with the need for white socks, thinking black was near enough. A couple of bucks a throw every time we had an official umpire to do the officious reporting—or even a vindictive opposing captain—was enough to keep us impoverished, and was our small contribution to the ongoing health of the Association.

The Association had another little earner requiring attendance by all clubs at the monthly meeting. By virtue of a local rule, never encountered in any other comp, all teams were required to use balls with the NCCCA crest stamped on them—which of course could only be purchased from the little man who sat all night at his table over to one side awaiting his moment of glory when everyone had to queue up to purchase, at prices appropriate to the Association's needs, their required stock of official competition balls.

My first acquaintance with the rule came in the first game in which I acted as captain of NOBs. We batted first against Thomastown United, and knocked up a couple of hundred before our innings closed with a good half hour to stumps on the first day. As we prepared ourselves for the field it crossed my mind to ask Pat, then Club Secretary, for the new ball. Immediate consternation. Pat's girlfriend, Pip (only girlfriends ever came to watch their men play—wives having long ago seen through the charade), had watched the first hour or so of the game, then driven off in search of better ways of filling in Saturday afternoon. The match ball was in the car, of course.

We rummaged through the kit, and not even knocked-about remnants of previous games were to be found. The only thing resembling a cricket ball was made of washed-out leather faded to a soft pink, which looked as if someone's dog had been chewing it all winter. It had the consistency of blancmange.

With this sorry excuse in my hand I was forced to approach the opposing captain to explain this was the only ball we had. With no optimism whatsoever I suggested maybe we could buy one of their balls. No, we couldn't. 'Anyway,' I said, 'there's nothing in the Laws of Cricket to say you have to use a new ball at the start of an innings.'

There was of course a bush lawyer in their team who was a jump ahead of me, and forcefully pointed out that, whatever the Laws of Cricket might say, there was a competition rule very clear about the fact that, at least at the start of an innings, the Association crest must be visible on any ball used in an official match. It had been a very long time since any gold lettering was visible on our ball.

This left us at an impasse. All I could say was that if they wanted the match points for a forfeit they could have them, and we'd get an early start in the pub and all next week off. If they wanted a game of cricket, we were prepared to make do with the sad relic.

They held a team meeting on the subject (I missed my chance to claim a forfeit on the grounds their batsmen were not on the field within ten minutes of the end of our innings) and, much against the audible protests of the bush lawyer, decided to play on. Their captain, by way of settling the issue, said to his antagonist, 'They won't get anyone out with that rag.'

Despite his confidence they were two down at stumps, and things were delicately poised for next week. We hadn't heard the last for the day from their expert on the rules. As we left the field he rushed up to his captain, one of the not out batsmen, and shouted at him, 'Sign the ball, sign the ball.' This was his way of ensuring we didn't slip in a newer, harder, more responsive item for the next week's play. A few biro scratches were duly made on the wilted leather and the ball was thrown forlornly into the kit.

At our regular pre-match gathering at the pub the following Saturday, one of the team, Bruce Mathiessen, decided to do what he could towards shining up the ball. It looked to me a useless endeavour, but it is amazing what large quantities of saliva and vigorous abrasion on shirt and strides can achieve. No illegal substances were used—just the old-fashioned way of shining the ball. After half an hour or so, one side of the ball had achieved a quite remarkable sheen.

Too late it occurred to me to ask which side of the ball he had been concentrating on. By then, the opposing captain's moniker was completely obliterated. I headed for the ground with a heavy heart. Though we knew it was the same ball, no one else in a position to make a comparison would ever believe it. It is not pleasant to be regarded as a cheat, and the circumstances were wholly damning.

In pre-match preparations there were no enquiries about the ball, and as we took the field I nursed hopes that we might get away with it. After two overs or so the superficial gloss would be gone, and a couple of compliments about the power of his off-drive might cajole the captain into believing his signature had been bashed off the ball.

I set the field (always the same one) and Clem was about to begin his run in when a familiar voice was raised from the boundary: 'Have you checked the ball?'

The captain, who was about to take strike, wasn't a bad bloke—certainly by comparison. He turned to the team huddle, waved his arm in contempt and shouted 'Yes'. The game resumed, Clem took six or seven, and we won by quite a few runs. The ball was quickly thrown into the deepest recesses of the kit, hands were shaken, and we headed back to the pub. Pat was congratulated for arranging for us to bowl with a ball so soft that no one could hit it to the boundary.

The next week he took us all to the wrong ground, ten miles from where we were supposed to be playing, and dissident voices began to mutter that perhaps Pat's organisational skills were on a par with his cricketing abilities. No more damning accusation could be made, and the next season, in a bloodless coup—probably organised by Pat himself—Geoff Crossman was installed as Secretary.

Soon after, in keeping with our new-found professionalism, we elevated Geoff from Secretary to General Manager—a distinction without a difference. A little more foresight and we could have made him Chief Executive Officer, thus leading the club into the brave new world of rationalisation that we did not quite survive to see.

There was one other position the precise function of which no amount of verbal tinkering could disguise, and from which no amount of conspiracy and manoeuvre could dislodge the incumbent—and that was the post usually known as Treasurer. Having cornered the job from the start, Ken Latta was immovable, since no one else had any idea where the club's assets were: Cayman Islands, the Bahamas, or perhaps on Number 6 in the last at Sandown.

The team's annual reports contained either a fog of detail no one could be bothered following, or a terse statement to the effect that 'the Club Treasurer assures us we're still solvent'.

But Ken, universally known as Legs,[4] demonstrated himself worthy of our implicit trust, not only by stumping up the cash whenever needed, but also, after the club had folded up altogether, letting the troops know that there was still a couple of hundred in the kitty, and we were going to cut it out over a long counter lunch.

Yarraville Football Club was the first organisation to exploit Legs' abilities to the full. As the designated representative whose task it was to explain to the Tribunal just why the reported player should be excused of whatever brutality he had been charged with, Legs had a spotless record—not a single suspension. Given the way Yarraville played—well, the whole of the VFA Second Division—this was an extraordinary achievement.[5]

His cricket was less distinguished, but had features which impressed themselves strongly upon the observer. Everything you hear or read about batsmanship centres on footwork, especially the importance of getting the front foot to the pitch of the ball.

---

4   Though this is not the actual explanation of the nickname, it seemed appropriate in that his talent for the game seemed to mark Legs out as one of nature's Number Elevens. This meant that in any normal NOBs line-up we could generally find two or three eminently qualified to bat below him.

This was advice which Legs had only half absorbed. He would advance his knees towards the line of the ball while leaving his feet exactly where they started. This graceful genuflection would bring his head to a point about six inches lower than his normal stance, with the weight of his upper body beginning to topple forward.

With his knees so far in advance of his shoulders, a free swing of the bat was next to impossible, so drives were out. His scoring range was limited to a quick motion of the bat across his nearly horizontal pads, shovelling the ball behind square leg—a manoeuvre at which he was surprisingly adept. Bowlers accustomed to a more orthodox approach grew frustrated at seeing deliveries wide of off stump being angled away to an unexpected part of the field, and loudly informed Legs what they thought of his methods.

Legs's response to these criticisms was generally along the lines that if he'd thought he was any good at the game he certainly wouldn't be playing at this level. The logic of this was sufficiently subtle to leave the bowler feeling that he didn't understand quite clearly enough to be able to formulate an answer, but pretty sure that he'd just lost the argument. For want of any other reply, he'd let one go around the ears; but since this was entirely to be expected anyway, no additional harm was done.

In the field Legs became well known among his team mates for the regularity with which he prostrated himself full length on the ground at the fall of a wicket, always facing away from our pitch, his attention apparently absorbed by the match on the ground next to us. On occasions when the fresh batsman was padded up and straining at

---

5   In fact the most entertaining piece of Tribunal behaviour in this period involved Yarraville only as the injured party. In 1979 they had demolished Sunshine by 20 goals. As their full forward lined up for his umpteenth goal, one of the Sunshine boys was reported for baring his buttocks. The defence at the Tribunal was that this was not an action designed to cause offence but merely a description of how the Yarraville player had been getting his goals all day. This judicious piece of impartial aesthetic commentary was not received by the Tribunal in the spirit it was offered, and the player was suspended for 10 matches.

the leash to get in and on with the contest, the captain would have to exhort his loafing troops, 'Batsman in, lads, on your feet.'

More than once Legs advised us from over his shoulder that the call of nature, which he was answering in discreet and gentlemanly fashion, was not yet satisfied. This would require the captain to indulge in earnest consultation with the bowler concerning the precise placing of the close-in catchers until Legs arose from his leisurely labours and let it be known that play could re-commence, receiving his full and much more relaxed attention.

Such were the personnel who guided our club's destiny. Everything about us bore witness to the inescapability of the law of entropy, the tendency of all forces to be random and all energy to run down. The condition of the gear we used, the principles of organisation on which we proceeded, the chaotic manner in which we scratched out an existence marked us out as a team that was not there for the long haul.

That we survived as long as we did is testimony to the restorative power of repeated draughts of ale, and to the (almost) endless enjoyment human beings can derive from witnessing the folly of their companions.

2

The Level Playing Field and Other Surfaces

Prince's Park lies between the suburbs of Carlton and Parkville, next to the Melbourne General Cemetery. The northern half of the park is occupied by the mushrooming stadium of the Carlton Football Club—no longer the lovely open ground it was when the Victorian Football League encouraged people to go to watch the game; now instead surrounded by gloomy barracks, full of seats no one is allowed to sit in, all built in a style that has been described as the Bulgarian school of architecture.

There are two spacious ovals to the south of the major compound, used by the second XIs of the University and Carlton Cricket Clubs, surrounded by white boundary fences, with carefully tended turf wickets—even a scoreboard if anyone can be bothered keeping it. Between these two well watered ovals lie several acres of flat, featureless ground, abundant with capeweed in the late spring, parched and arid by February. This area is an overflow carpark for the footy season, but the domain of desperately eager park cricketers in the summer.

Except for a brief period where we were dislodged by elephants (see below), NOBs' home turf (or home matting, to be strictly accurate) was always in Prince's Park, though with the passage of years and the dwindling of clubs using the park, we graduated from a clapped-out asphalt track in the bottom corner to a concrete pitch on the eastern fringe, and finally to one on the western flank, where the graceful trees that line Royal Parade provide welcome shade, and the scorers do not have to sit all afternoon gazing straight into the lowering summer sun.

Prince's Park was a relatively level and true playing surface— considerable virtues in park cricket. Orrong Park, the home ground of my B grade team in South Suburban Churches (a much higher standard of competition) dropped perhaps twenty feet from the southern end to the northern, and was so narrow that there was a ground rule that the boundary from wide mid-off to third man on both sides counted three only.

Our fast bowler, The Slug, once demonstrated the extra excitement that such a rule can add to the game. He was fielding just in front of point when the ball was played square of him. In a desperate effort to intercept he lunged at it with his left foot, alas a fraction too late to make a stop but perfect timing for a drop kick. The ball consequently careered off down the hill at right angles to its original course, crossing the four boundary behind the slips sixty or seventy yards from the three boundary at point, for which it was originally headed.

Without even a boundary fence to separate Orrong Park from the adjoining Prahran High School, our ground was effectively though not legally a school oval, being used on weekdays as part of the recreational area. This is not unusual, as park cricket frequently makes use of the resources of our state's public education institutions in order to find a home and a haven. Occasionally, however, weekend recreation and educational activity find themselves at cross-purposes.

Having effected illicit entry into the small, shabby, corrugated-iron shed that served as our changing rooms and storage area for the club mats, some students of a more enquiring disposition used the facilities to broaden their knowledge of life. In the innocence of those long-gone days, no one who picked up the mats to cart them out to the middle had to worry about needle-stick injury, pre-owned condoms being a more marginal hazard. But it is as certain as such things can be that it was a post-coital cigarette, carelessly discarded on the mats that helped to transform the concrete floor into a bower of bliss, that caused the fire that destroyed the shed and burned the mats, and forced us to unwelcome expense before we were able to host our next home game.

Unwary cricketers can sometimes find themselves in trouble when making use of these grounds that belong to public institutions—as demonstrated by the social game (not one in which NOBs participated) arranged at a ground that turned out to be within the precinct of the old Kew Mental Hospital. Early arrivals were particularly pleased with the pretty outlook and the well-kept ground that awaited them, and were accordingly most complimentary to the resident responsible for its upkeep, who in his turn was anxious to secure the approval of the visitors.

In an impulsive but ill-considered act of gratitude, one of them made him a present of three bottles of beer. Sudden second thoughts suggested this had not been the wisest course of action, but it seemed both too late and too churlish to ask for them back. With a slight air of panic, and probably only compounding the original error of judgement, he said, 'You won't tell anyone, will you?' To which the honorary groundsman replied, 'What do you think I am, completely mad or something?'

Park cricket is forced to make do with whatever sort of space can be found. Sometimes a club will be lucky enough to secure a small park where their pitch is the only one, the odd tree inside the playing arena and a short boundary on one side for the benefit of the blind slogger being normal defects of such grounds, along with certain undulations, which can be attractive for landscaping purposes but dangerous to sportsmen.

A sudden steep slope approaching the boundary can surprise an unwary chaser. On one ground at Bundoora the council had thoughtfully cut into the natural slope to give a level surface, so that for some distance the boundary consisted of a stone retaining wall, with unfortunate consequences for one of our number, Mark McPherson.

The sole redeeming feature of Mark's cricket was an abundance of enthusiasm. However hopeless the chase, his zeal in pursuit never flagged, leaving older members shaking their heads. This day at Bundoora he set off as usual, head down, knees pumping. His spatial sense was not that of a born athlete, and his collision with the wall could have resulted in a fractured skull or worse. It was fortunate emergency assistance was not required, since the rest of the team, rolling in mirth, was incapable of providing it. Stunned as he was, he was still the first one back on his feet.

Such highly engineered structures were unusual on the grounds we inhabited. More characteristic of park cricket in general is the large treeless area with its warren of concrete pitches laid down like a jig-saw across broad parkland, such as NOBs called 'home'. Sometimes there will be changing sheds doing duty for perhaps eight or ten grounds, but probably over the other side of the park, so the back seat of the car is more convenient—or better still the open air. The total absence of spectators—for no one would settle down to watch a contest played at this level—means that the modesty of only the odd passing jogger is likely to be offended by the dropping and raising of drawers and the various fumbling adjustments the game requires before one sallies forth to battle.

Immediately adjoining our original pitch was another urban feature familiar to park cricketers—a small brick Gents toilet block. Like most such public conveniences it extended its aura for some distance, acrid enough to indicate that it was still serving the function originally intended, though the abundance of forlorn sexual implorings scribbled on the walls suggested that the counter-culture had other uses for it.

No one ever got changed in there—whether from the smell, or the fear of assaults on our masculine virginity. Not much to worry about really. We were not an attractive lot, and anyway the graffitists stayed away of a Saturday afternoon, probably aware that, at least in its public presentation, park cricket is assertively heterosexual. The spirit of the New Age did not breathe upon the Northern and Combined Churches.

Away games took us to a variety of widely scattered venues, a few close-handy but most of them (as the association's name indicated) in the sometimes depressing suburbs of Melbourne's north. Some grounds, like Donath Reserve in Thomastown to which we were drawn a couple of times a season, contained several overlapping grounds (and a central toilet block), rather resembling Prince's Park — if you took away the tall trees and the cemetery. There were school grounds like Lalor High, where negligent mowers gave us an utterly undeserved victory[1], green belt areas on the fringes of the Yarra,

---

1   See page 45–46.

where historic events fell upon us[2], and pleasant parks like the Edinburgh Gardens, which, arched by ancient elms and fringed by gracious terrace houses, almost made you feel you were playing on the English village green—except that the fast bowlers' vocabulary may have had a slightly different tinge. Once we had to play in Epping, a region seldom visited by denizens of the central city like us. 'How do you get there?' someone asked, to which the most useful answer was, 'Catch the train to Albury and walk back.'

Across the broad swathe of northern Melbourne, cricket of a Saturday arvo has to compete with more traditional pursuits, such as revving the engine and filling the balmy summer air with the aroma of burning rubber. Just getting to the ground was often a hair-raising experience, and many a fine snick to the keeper was lost in the deafening roar of the neighbourhood taking its weekend relaxation.

A petrol-sodden afternoon was usually followed by a beer-sodden evening in one of the genial watering-holes like the Crock—and if you couldn't slap up a fight there in half an hour you just weren't trying. These social patterns partly explained our loyalty to Naughton's and our anxiety to get back there as soon as possible after the drawing of stumps. Some opponents hospitably invited us for a post-match beer, and a few quiet cans in the West Lalor club rooms could be very welcome, but the local pubs were not to our taste, and in any case the prevalence of Salvation Army teams meant the temptations were few.

If the undulating bass of souped-up jalopies formed a constant background noise, other sounds too dominated over the mellow thwack of leather on willow that is traditionally associated with the English version of the game. For Australian cricket is a hubbub of invective and excoriation. Every delivery and every shot is praised or ridiculed from both sides of the boundaries. 'Let's have another wicket—bowl him a piano, see if he can play that—knock his castle over—knock his bloody head off .' The variety is by no means end-

---

2   See Chapter 4.

less, but it is incessant. 'Too good for him!' chorus the slips and keeper for every ball that gets past the bat, no matter how far out of reach. At the same time, the non-striker might approvingly comment 'Well left,' even if the ball has missed the outside edge by a hair's breadth. 'Let that rubbish go, wait till he puts one on the stumps,' echoes from the boundary.

One in particular of our regular opponents, Thomastown United, believed that constant verbal urging was an essential part of the game. If you couldn't think of anything to say yourself, you could at least encourage others to keep up the barrage. The oval resounded with the cry, 'Talk it up, 'Towers, talk it up!' And talk it up they did, without pause. Just occasionally some of the more metaphorical members of the team would embellish with, 'Talk it up, 'Towers, this ain't no turkey shoot!'—a phrase whose Australian origins are open to doubt.

More direct and personal abuse was, of course, part and parcel of the game, and followed every incident—a dropped catch, an appeal turned down, a mis-hit stroke—with an intensity that belied our nominal affiliation with the Christian Church.

As for the playing arenas themselves, the pitches upon which we did battle usually observed the recommended north–south alignment, though sometimes oddly skewed into the setting sun, but whoever positioned them did so with scant regard to the fact that while the game is in progress the fieldsmen are required to spread themselves over a considerable area. A boundary sixty or so yards from your own pitch may run straight through the centre of the next wicket, requiring outfielders to pay as much attention to the adjoining game as to their own. Standing with your back to a batsman only twenty yards away can be a painful experience.

On one occasion the Club Founder, Pat O'Connor, was fielding on the midwicket boundary when the ball was hit hard and flat in his direction. NOBs must have been doing poorly, because Pat's attention was entirely occupied by the game on the next, and much nearer, pitch, when he was awakened by the shouts of his team-mates. He turned round with the ball only yards from him and approaching rapidly. Awareness of danger can arouse profound instincts. It was perhaps no more than an involuntary gesture to protect his face, but Pat thrust up his hands and caught the ball. He was no odds-on to catch it if he'd been watching, so that may have been the way to go.

Unfortunately, future experiments in forgetting which game he was playing in never achieved a similar success, such as the occasion in the Grand Final where he was sent down to the long on boundary, where the low-order slogger had just whacked a couple. The very next ball was lifted straight to him and safely caught, at which point Pat raised both arms to signify six. Not being on the field of play at all is generally considered a tactical disadvantage in taking up a fielding position.

Pat was, however, responsible for an exciting innovation in the presentation of the game, on a par with the dog track at the Gabba or the movable rope at the MCG. He decided the club could do with a new and unique set of boundary markers.

It is almost unknown for park cricket grounds to have a boundary fence, so the perimeter must be marked with flags. This is the responsibility of the home team, and the job is sometimes performed by eye and judgement, which is a frequent cause of arguments about why the flags are more or less distant on the second Saturday, depending on whether the home side is bowling or batting. A length of string is handy, but not infallible since no one ever checks to make sure it's fully rolled out.

Most park clubs in our time had a couple of dozen well-worn scraps of coloured cloth tacked onto pointed sticks a foot or so long that could be poked into the ground to mark the boundary, although now these seem to have given way to snazzy little plastic cones. There is a strict rule in all competitions that the real boundary is a straight line between the flags, to prevent niggardly fieldsmen drawing a broad arc around them so as to say it wasn't four. But who is on the spot to check? The honour system prevails, which is both the blessing and the curse of park cricket.

Patrick sought something more sturdy and durable than the conventional flag, and he had the means of production at hand—his Year 9 metalwork class. It is clear that this was an entirely appropriate expenditure of Education Department funds, as it familiarised his students with the basic shape of the triangle and taught them both the strength of a weld and the superior virtues of a pointed stake when it comes to sticking things in the ground.

Though the substitute flags stood out proudly from the masthead on even windless days, there were two major drawbacks to their use. One was that Pat had painted them an unusual shade of blue which, though very distinctive when viewed on its own, happened to be, in one of those freaks of nature, a perfect camouflage for the colour of the ground. Even when carefully turned side-on they were extremely difficult to pick out, and at the end of the day it was not uncommon for those collecting the flags to come back one or two short because they simply hadn't seen them as they walked the boundary.

A more serious objection was that the sheet metal used was lethally sharp at the point of the triangle, and a fieldsman in hot pursuit could easily have laid his shin open on them. Even pulling them out of the ground or carrying an armful of them was a delicate operation.

By conventional usage, where grounds overlap the flags are laid flat (difficult to manage with your modern plastic cones), so as not to impede the fieldsmen in the adjoining game. This made our flags rather like landmines, utterly invisible until they were trodden on, at which point they would fly into the air, threatening life and limb. More than once fieldsmen in the next game were seen to hurl these spiteful little objects as far from their own pitch as they could, thus somewhat defeating the purpose of marking the boundary in the first place.

So it became necessary to rummage in the kit to find the scruffy old cloth flags and donate Patrick's invention to the nearest abattoir.

The risk of being struck on the back of the scone by a ball from the next game, or impaled on your own flags was not the only physical danger to which we were exposed. The condition of the ground itself was often a major hazard.

Some of us of more mature years fielded only with reluctance before Christmas. At this time of year the capeweed is still luxuriant and the surface particularly slow. A ball struck wide of the field needs to be chased all the way to the boundary, and the exertion required can seriously impair one's dignity. However, since no sensible Council wastes precious water on grounds used for park cricket, after Christmas when the capeweed dies off the grounds are like lightning. A shot straight to you might be stopped, but if it is wide of you it is four without a doubt, and a gentle trot after the ball is all that is required— or even just a loud 'Hoy!' to the fieldsmen in the game next door to warn them of the approach of an adventitious object. (It is always nice to be able to throw the ball back to the neighbouring game. It gives one a sense, however mistaken and however brief, that someone else is getting a worse shellacking than you are.)

Some grounds, however, dry out to such an extent that huge cracks open up, some large enough to swallow a ball and most guaranteed to cause alarming deviations in even a gently played stroke. A ball struck powerfully along the ground can suddenly take off three feet in front of you, heading straight for the face.

Cricket coaches are forever telling their young charges to get the body behind the ball, and to keep the eye on the ball all the way.

Where we played, the first piece of advice was not always easy to follow, since the ball could suddenly head away at a remarkable angle. The second was potentially dangerous, and it was always advisable to turn the head away for safety's sake.

One particular member of NOBs, Shane Ryan, possessed a rare talent for getting a bad bounce. Being of very thin build, he seemed all angles and no matter where the ball struck him it seemed to catch a protruding bone. The very gentlest shots would see him wringing his hands or rubbing his shins, but his hallmark performance came one day when fielding in the covers. The ball was hit firmly to his left, but not so firmly that it should have presented a challenge to an average C-grade cricketer. But Shane was no average C-grader. He made a couple of half-hearted strides towards it before withdrawing both body and hands in an exaggerated movement. 'Too good for me,' he was heard to mutter, as he turned to fetch the ball.

After this memorable event, 'Too good for me!' became a catch-cry within the club whenever the reward seemed not quite worth the effort.

Lest it be thought, however, that Shane's commitment to the game was not deeply serious, one story should rescue his reputation. An Old Boy of Assumption College, Kilmore, of around Shane's vintage has informed us of a recent school reunion where the calm of genial reminiscence was jarred by a spirited argument between Shane and one of his contemporaries about exactly which one of them (both now comfortably in their fifties) had been responsible for the confusion leading to one of them being run out in the under-elevens. 'He that filches from me my good name/ Robs me of that which not enriches him/ And makes me poor indeed.' And Shane was always one of those who hotly contested whether or not a particular dropped catch should be counted against his name.

Shane's most spectacular fielding performance actually occurred once while he was waiting to bat. The first innings of both sides had been concluded with an hour or so of the second Saturday to spare. Our opponents insisted on playing on to the death, though no out-right result was remotely possible. NOBs were more than a little an-noyed at being denied an early start in the pub, but had to begin our second innings. We therefore decided to do nothing at all to make things easy for the fielding side, like throwing the ball back to them if a boundary was hit near where we were all sitting.

Sure enough, one of the batsmen cracked a mighty shot in our direction, which promised to run on for a considerable distance and give one of the opposition a very long chase. As we parted ranks and turned to watch its rapid career, we saw Shane, all padded up and pacing nervously ten yards or so behind us, go down on one knee to field the ball. Someone called out to him to let it go, and remember-ing the team plan, he jumped to get out of the way. But as he did so his feet went from under him, and he did a belly flopper straight on top of the ball. He landed on it not only with his midsection but with the abdominal protector itself, which was driven hard against his vitals, bringing tears to not only his eyes but those of everyone around.

Some unevenness of ground must also have been the cause of Geoff Crossman's famous fall, an earth-shattering event that occurred at Donath Reserve in Thomastown.

Unlike Shane, Geoff was built on generous lines and his method of running could best be described as scudding. On this occasion he turned to chase the ball with a flurry of arms and legs, but it was soon apparent to the rest of the team that he was in serious trouble. Those who saw it were agreed that it resembled nothing so much as a slow-motion film of an airliner disintegrating, as various sections seem to peel off. The first to go was his cap, followed by a boot and sock, each describing a lazy arc above his head. Somewhere in there his pants fell down, revealing a hairy and not altogether attractive back-side. It took at least fifteen yards from the point at which instability set in, stubby legs pounding faster but shorter by the stride, to where he finally struck the earth in a cloud of dust, shirt bursting at the seams in the process.

As he picked himself up and gathered himself together, the batsmen continued to run doggedly between the wickets. With insufficient feeling for the big man's humiliation I urged him to throw the ball in. He replied in a voice full of disdain, 'It's f———— four,' and flipped the ball in underhand. The ball was returned to the bowler, Max Radcliffe, who carefully placed it on the ground at the end of his run before lying prostrate in order to cope with the paroxysms of mirth convulsing him.

Amidst the general hilarity of the NOBs the two batsmen solemnly exhorted each other, 'Don't let them break your concentration.'—as if the whole event had been carefully choreographed to achieve a tactical advantage. Not all teams approached the game in the spirit that NOBs did.

One random element to do with ground conditions that can affect the course of a game is the length of the grass. Since most games take place over two Saturdays there can be a decided but unpredictable advantage. Or perhaps not entirely unpredictable. One regular of Naughton's public bar was Charlie Doherty, who drove a mower for the Melbourne City Council. If we were playing at home, Charlie would always ask if we were batting next Saturday so he'd know whether or not to put the mower over the ground.

In a hot summer there is no grass at all after Christmas, so it would have made no difference whether Charlie was at work or not, but we did win one game solely on the length of the grass—although the mowing was entirely out of our control.

It was the first of many games we played against West Lalor Cricket Club, this one on the school oval at Lalor High—many miles outside the boundaries of the Melbourne City Council. When we arrived for the game the grass was shin high. The spin of the coin went our way, and we invited the home side to bat.

All day, sixes were easier to hit than fours. It was impossible to reach the boundary with a ball struck along the ground. The few that were scored for the afternoon were all first bounce over. Any more, and they stopped dead. Their 110 for the day was worth far more than double that. The main concern in placing the field was to have sufficient coverage so that the ball didn't get lost in the grass.

We arrived for the second Saturday to find the grass neatly mown and raked, and everything set up for batting. After a long struggle with nine wickets down, and a very dodgy 'not out' with the last man in, we sneaked past their score by 1.

West Lalor rightly felt somewhat aggrieved by this ill-fortune— not to mention what they regarded as a bit of straight-out cheating— and sought revenge. They did not have long to wait, since by a quirk of the competition the club had two teams playing in the same grade. Their firsts were in A grade, or perhaps B, but both their seconds and thirds were in D grade. Not only that, but, having embarrassed ourselves in victory over their thirds, we were to play their seconds next match. This match took place on their altogether superior ground round the corner at Huskisson Reserve—not only a broad and flat playing surface but, greatest of rarities at our level of park cricket, a fence around the boundary. And neatly mown grass.

The two bowlers who had done so much damage to our batting the week before, Dirty and Smelly (West Lalor were a team of nick- names, none of them complimentary) had earned themselves promo- tion for their efforts. They were the only two bowlers the thirds had, so they bowled all afternoon, and very well too. To our great good fortune the captain of the seconds thought they were third and fourth change in his line-up, and by the time they got the ball NOBs were away to a flyer. Dirty and Smelly brought things back into order when they got the chance, but 260 was always going to be hard to make, and we won the game handsomely.

A spacious ground with no interference from neighbouring pitches, comfortable changing rooms and even a fridge for the after-match beer—it was almost like serious cricket. On this occasion at least it brought out the best in NOBs, by contrast with some of the performances we put in on our own pitch.

There was an extenuating reason for our indifferent batting at home. Our original pitch was an ancient asphalt one that was beginning to break up, with the occasional tuft of grass growing through it. The surface was wickedly uneven and no amount of stretching the mats could iron out its irregularities. The fastest bowler I ever faced in that competition, known by friend and foe as The Beast, was particularly fearsome on it, and I recall Geoff Crossman struck in the throat from a well-pitched ball, then getting right in behind the next one, which seemed particularly courageous at the time—especially as we were a helmetless team in those pre-gladiatorial days.

Pat O'Connor, then Club Secretary, had in fact done his best to spare us this life-threatening confrontation by informing everyone that we were playing at Kingsbury Tech, ten miles to the north. When we arrived we found two pitches, and four teams already assembled, none of which was the team we were supposed to be playing. Someone suggested we consult the fixture list, which required a hasty scramble to collect the mats and the flags and get back to Prince's Park, where the match got underway very late, due to the courtesy of our opponents, who could certainly have claimed a forfeit.

After this initial encounter with The Beast on a surface giving him plenty of help, there were voices raised in the pub that night that we'd have been better off staying at Kingsbury Tech for the afternoon. The condition of the pitch led us to appeal to the City Council for better treatment, and we were eventually promoted to a concrete pitch of much better quality, though one that possessed hazards of an entirely different order.

This was the occasion when one of the troops arrived at Naughton's before the game (it being our habit to assemble at the pub before as well as after play—just a small hair-of-the-dog to stiffen the resolve) and asked if we'd seen what was going on at the ground. What he had to report was so astonishing that we immediately forsook our pre-match preparation and migrated the half-mile to our pitch in Prince's Park, where we watched as the crew completed the erection of a huge circus tent on our ground. The area around about a good length at the southern end of the pitch was knee-deep in elephant dung.

It is a formidable and time-consuming feat of engineering to raise a structure of that kind, and those in charge of the operation showed no willingness at all to fold their battered caravanserai in favour of a motley collection of park cricketers, whose drawing power as a public spectacle was certainly inferior to their own. And they of course had a Council permit to use the space, just as we did.

We didn't seriously consider debating the issue with them. Their possession of numerous sledgehammers and the brawn required to bash in the many large tent pegs that were part of their trade tipped the balance decisively in their favour. That, and a certain gypsy solidarity that did not look kindly on our frivolously aristocratic way of spending a Saturday afternoon. Anyway, any attempt on our part to move them on would have run into a major problem, since our team did not include anyone with much idea of how to drive an elephant.

The visit of the circus so close to the heart of the city had more serious repercussions for another acquaintance of ours. Bobbo was never a NOB, but was close enough to our drinking circle to have once purchased from me what turned out to be the winning ticket in a club raffle. Since the prize was 200 cans of beer, I took it as a genuine sign of friendship that he agreed that the ticket seller had the right to share a significant portion of the winnings.

During the week of the circus he was carousing in one of the Carlton pubs, and at closing time found himself in the company of a lone member of the troupe who had broken ranks for a night on the tiles but was now lamenting that the doors of the boarding house would all be locked.

Bobbo's magnanimity in offering a roof for the night was somewhat mitigated by the fact that the only sleeping room available—at least to someone thinking as clearly as he was at the time—was in the bath. However generous his initial impulse, it was clearly unwise not to have woken his wife to inform her of their visitor, since it came as a considerable shock to her, when she arose for her morning shower, to find a female dwarf asleep in the bath. This left Bobbo with even more explaining than we had had to do on the preceding Saturday.

Fairfield Salvation Army had been our opponents only one season earlier—that time on their home ground, in the match recorded in Chapter 4 that culminated in a cameo appearance on national television—so they knew from experience that games against NOBs could provide unexpected variety. On this occasion, having been alerted to the unusual goings on at the ground, we were for once in attendance well before the scheduled start of play, though we had of course done nothing about laying the mats and setting out the flags. As the opposition arrived in dribs and drabs we were there to greet them, though we couldn't offer much by way of explanation except the obvious fact that there was a circus on our ground.

Fairfield seemed to accept that this was an occurrence beyond our control, and not something you would naturally predict and take precautions against. It was agreed that NOBs contact the Council to find another ground on which we could play a one-day game the next Saturday, which is what happened eventually, though not without an intervening complication.

Some of our team were familiar with some members of the opposition; friends at school, in fact. In the course of making our arrangements for the following week, mention was made of the monthly meeting of the Association, which was due to take place on the coming Monday. Fairfield's delegate to the meeting—let us call him Eric, for that was indeed his name—was without transport to this summit of cricket's powerbrokers in the northern suburbs. As he lived quite close to our delegate, Geoff Crossman, he asked if he could get a lift to the bleak church hall where these purgatorial events took place. Geoff was happy to agree, and duly picked up his opposite number.

When Geoff reported next Friday training session what had happened at the meeting, even such jaded cynics as NOBs were taken by surprise. There was always an item on the agenda in which the President asks if there is any business concerning matches in progress. At this point Eric had jumped to his feet and asked that Fairfield Salvos be awarded a forfeit on the basis that we, as home team, had not provided a ground for the match to take place. After Geoff explained the circumstances and the verbal agreement with our opponents, the Association wisely ruled in our favour. Official endorsement did not prevent Geoff from repeating his views even more forcefully to Eric after the meeting was over, with the sad consequence that Eric had to walk home that night.

There are lessons here with which every park cricketer ought to be conversant: whether you are playing at home or away, organise your own transport, and never trust the opposition to do the decent thing.

3

Ring-ins and Recruits

In an efficiently run cricket club there are keen contenders striving
for promotion to the senior team, or just to get a game at any level.
Net practice sees the younger players eagerly trying to catch the eye
of the selectors, while veterans on the slide chat up their old mates
on the panel, calling in favours in the hope that recent performances
might be overlooked.

As a one-team club in the lower reaches of a matting competition,
and one that had dispensed with anything so vigorous as practice
sessions, NOBs organised itself rather differently. Of necessity, the
eleven to take the field was sorted out in the public bar on Friday

evening, and comprised the rag-tag regulars and a couple of desperates rounded up at closing time to swell the numbers.

The highly problematic composition of the side made it impossible to comply on every occasion with the rules of the Association concerning registration of players. The best we could do was to make sure we had enough names on the list to cover eventualities. That is, we resorted habitually to the honourable Australian tradition of the ring-in.

In reconstructing the history of the club's on-field deeds, old score books are of limited value since the names recorded bear no strict relationship to the players who actually took part. An alarming inconsistency in the performances of some team members can be explained by the discrepant abilities of the various impostors who took on that identity.

Having been myself a Friday night recruit, I can record the authentic experience of turning up on an uncertain Saturday afternoon at a ground near enough to the pub but only vaguely designated, apprehensively encountering a clutch of scruffy sportsmen, some of whom were vaguely familiar from the previous night's carousing. I was introduced in perfunctory fashion to a number of people whose names were immediately lost in the mists of the night before, and told that for the purposes of the day my name was Craig Price.

This match was the occasion of an epic NOBs disaster, which will be faithfully recorded elsewhere, but at the close of the first day's play I found myself taking off the pads as one of the not out batsmen. A wicket had fallen in the last over, and the scorebook attendant had not caught up with the incoming batsman.

The opposing captain, rightly sensing that an outright win was in prospect on the second Saturday of the game, was anxious that the exact state of play should be properly recorded in the book. Arguments about who'd bowled the last over from which end the week before, or even why the not out batsman was somewhat taller and facing up left-handed this week when he'd batted right-handed last Saturday, are not unknown at this level of cricket.

Quite reasonably, the captain came over to where we were taking off our pads and asked our names. Somewhere in the day's hectic events I had lost track of my supposed identity, so I said nothing, confident that my partner, who was the incoming batsman, and whose name therefore would be the missing one, would supply the necessary information. What I did not know was that my partner, to whom I had been introduced at the start of the day as Kevin Brown, was also a first gamer, playing under the name of Gerry Beaton, a fact of which he had as little recall as I did of my alias.

So when we were asked our names, neither of us knew, a confusion difficult to conceal. Rather too late it occurred to me to suggest that all communications should be directed through the captain, but such high principled recourse to the Laws of Cricket seemed an inadequate response to being caught with, so to speak, one's pads down.

Even in my first game with the club, I should have realised that constant practice in illegal substitutions had not actually given us any skill in the art.

The following season I played under my own name, and bequeathed the eternal resurrection of Craig Price[1] to another intruder. In the second game of the season a couple of mates of Crossman's decided to have a hit, so one of them — Steve Loney — was given the Price tag. No one was full bottle on the rules of the Association, but it turned out that at the start of the season you were given several weeks' grace on registration, so someone could play and then get his name on the books afterwards. Steve did pretty well in that game, making

---

1 There was a genuine Craig Price who played in NOBs's inaugural game, and never thereafter. He remained, however, an indispensable stand-by for seasons to come, lending his identity to numerous ring-ins. The real Gerry Beaton played several times, though irregularly. A tattooed fast bowler, he was the terror of umpires and the club treasurer alike. Not one to tolerate contradiction by a white-clad official, he always spoke his mind. The huddled slips field and wicketkeeper kept a running count of the likely fines with each unsuccessful appeal Gerry made.

runs and taking wickets, so we made the most of this opportunity to register him (under his baptismal name) for the season.

But at the same time we were informed that the draw had been changed (another story in itself) and we were going to play the same team next up. It seemed prudent to play him under the same name, as he would certainly be recognised by the opposition. The practice became habit, and he played the full season as Craig Price. It is probably unique in Australian sporting history that a player should compete as a ring-in when formally registered under his own name. What is certain is that it was the most successful season Craig Price ever enjoyed for the club, sharing the new ball with success and adding strength to the middle order.

In retrospect it seems a pity we did not think to consummate our personnel policy in an elegant fashion by playing one of our many ring-ins that season as Steve Loney, while the real Steve Loney played under a pseudonym.

A later incarnation of Craig Price occurred when Les Twentyman, a figure notable in the public life of Melbourne, but certainly not for reasons related to cricket, played his one game for the NOBs. Les proudly proclaimed his Western Suburbs affiliation by sporting the thinnest of white shirts, which failed utterly to conceal the navy blue singlet underneath. After team sheets had been exchanged, Geoff Crossman, who was Club Secretary, enquired under what name we'd rung Les in. I told him 'Craig Price', and he informed me that for the first time in the club's history the name had not been registered that season. Deception has reached beyond cunning when even the ring-in name is illegal.

'Be sure your sins will find you out,' my parents told me all my youth, but the experience of the NOBs suggests that you can actually get away with an amazing amount without anyone waking up to what you're doing, as in the introduction of Mick Butera to the team.

On this particular Saturday afternoon it was obvious we were going to be a man short. Either one of the Friday night round-up had let us down, or the selection committee had extended their deliberations so close to closing time that they had lost the power of counting up to eleven.

To try to make good the numbers, Max Radcliffe headed off with a pocketful of two bobs for a few phone calls, in response to which, at no notice whatsoever, Mario ('Call me Mick') Butera duly arrived.

Hasty consultations took place, as a result of which it was decided to play him under the name Michael Sandy, which was a perfectly in-order name—even though designed for a different person altogether. I was particularly pleased with this innocent deception, as his preferred nickname already equipped him for the first half, and if someone were to query why such an unmistakably Mediterranean countenance should be sporting such an Anglo moniker, we could always plead a spelling mistake and say it should be Sandi.

The game was duly conducted (a thumping defeat) and no awkward questions arose. The next match it seemed we were going to be short again. One reason for this was that it was the first week of the finals, and since no one had thought we would be in contention some of the regulars had made other plans. So the last-minute substitution of the week before was repeated, and Mick took his place again.

As it turned out, our opponents were to be East Thomastown, the same team we had played the match before, so Mick would have to play under the same name. If for no other reason, Mick had made himself memorable to the opposition by being the third member of a hat trick captured by their fast bowler, aptly nicknamed The Beast. (I had modestly performed the median role in this event.)

So it was Michael Sandy once again. Unfortunately, there was a competition rule (designed to prevent clubs stacking their lower grade teams who had made the finals with A and B players if those sides had missed the finals) that to be eligible for a finals match a player must have appeared in three games during the regular season. The real Michael Sandy had played at least four games that year, except that all but one of these had been played under a false name, so whether as an alias or the real thing Michael Sandy was technically ineligible for the game.

Rain forced an early end, and East Thomastown, who had the match handsomely in hand anyway, rightly proceeded to the Grand Final by virtue of their higher position on the ladder. Since we did not manage to do anything to disturb the proper course of events, no one in the opposing camp was moved to scrutinise team lists and query the result.

Our habitual recourse to illegal substitutions was aided by the fact that Melbourne is a big enough city to give a reasonable guarantee of anonymity, but in a regional competition there is some slight risk of recognition, as happened on at least two occasions. A future stalwart of the club had played his first few games without incident before one of the opposition said, 'Why's he down in the book as John French? That's Bob Speechley.' It appeared he had worked with Bob a few years earlier and knew perfectly well who he was.

Max Radcliffe's response to this was to say it was a hyphenated name, Speechley-French, and he used the second half at week-ends. Apart from its utter improbability and its failure to explain why he should also change from Bob to John off-duty, the bare-faced lie struck some of us as demeaning to a team that had always indulged in higher standards of deceit.

The other occasion took us back to our origins at Northcote High School. Always hard-pressed to make up the eleven, we were occasionally forced to play someone who could only appear on the first day of the game. Once this was my mate Graham Baird, over from New Zealand for Christmas, due to return midweek. The holiday season had thinned our ranks, so, on the basis that ten and a half was better than ten, Graham was to play the first week.

The name Bernie O'Brien seemed to me a reasonable enough one to resort to, and I duly entered it on the team sheet. As I was exchanging lists with the opposing captain, he was loud in his greeting of several of our team. It turned out they'd all been within a year of each other at Northcote High. Furthermore, the real Bernie O'Brien, NOBs first captain indeed, was a teacher at Northcote High. The captain looked down our team list and said enthusiastically, 'I'm glad Bernie's playing. I haven't seen him since I left school.'

It seemed unlikely that we would be able to persuade him that in four or five years Bernie's flaming red beard had transformed itself into Graham's shaggy black one, not to speak of other dissimilarities of physique, which necessitated a re-think of our game plan. So a few minutes later I went up to the overly familiar opponent and told him that we'd just got word that Bernie couldn't play, but Don Cameron, who could only make it for the first week happened to be there, so could we substitute him for Bernie? 'He is properly registered?' he asked me, and on receiving my assurance on that point, agreed to the change. Don Cameron was indeed registered, but the man who played, Graham Baird, certainly was not.

Fiddling with team sheets turned out to be a mere peccadillo compared to other events during this match, when NOBs touched the hem of history and was catapulted onto the television screens of Australia that very day. But more of that in its proper place.

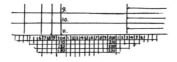

It is entirely possible that the reason why no opposition team ever challenged the composition of our team was that they were up to the same tricks as us and equally anxious to avoid close scrutiny of team lists. I find it hard to believe, however, that any other club created such difficulties for itself out of what should have been a fairly straightforward piece of deception.

The Speechley episode, which was the only time a member of the opposition caught us comprehensively in the act, passed without further consequences. Perhaps (though unlikely) the ingenuous opponent even believed Max's explanation. But from time to time the Association, nervous in principle about pub teams in a Churches competition (with good reason—see the chapter on The Royal Oak), took an undue interest in us. Though we were entirely innocent of the hooligan behaviour they feared, we were grateful that they neglected to examine the composition of the team.

The truth of the matter is NOBs's demeanour on the field was never of a kind to justify any alarm. Indeed we regarded ourselves as a civilising influence in the competition. Our infractions had nothing to do with unsporting behaviour or an over-committed zeal for victory, but rather consisted of a flagrant disregard for the formalities of the competition. As such, however, they were certainly serious enough to have earned us expulsion if they had been enquired into.

The possibility of such consequences was once raised—by, as it happens, the Club Philosopher, Dr Barry Taylor, a scholar whose international reputation in his field owes nothing to his dedicated problem-solving on our behalf.

For reasons utterly beyond our control—probably the disintegration and abandonment of other clubs even more disorganised than ours—NOBs were promoted from D grade to C. This caused immediate alarm among the ageing tosspots who sought some way of staying at a level of competition where they bowled just that little bit slower. The Club Philosopher was asked for an opinion. He contemplated the matter sagely for some time and then suggested, 'Why don't you tell them what you've been up to with ring-ins all these years and get yourselves kicked out of the whole competition?'

One sensible way round the problem would have been to sign up some blokes who were actually going to play, including some with a bit of ability, but we were loath to go talent scouting if it required a protracted absence from the public bar, so the available pool was a shallow and somewhat sticky one.

Even so, one talented cricketer did find himself in our company as a result of his social habits. A familiar Australian phrase represents the drinking man as 'propping up the bar'. Of Peter Horsburgh it could more accurately be said that his ample girth constituted a substantial chock for Carlton and United Breweries. I can recall coming into the bar one Friday and happily accepting Peter's offer of a beer. After a couple of rounds I'd sorted who was in the shout and bought my round in turn. As I passed Horsburgh his beer I noticed with surprise that, though he showed no signs of unaccustomed dallying over his drink, he still had a full pot in front of him. I asked him if he was drinking in two schools, to which he replied with an expression of great contentment, 'Yep. Plus I'm having one on my own.'

In his (presumably) slimmer youth he had played highly competitive cricket, representing Victorian Country at schoolboy level. The form guide and a cold beer had long since replaced his youthful enthusiasms, but as acquaintance grew—and with it a fair bit of late night boasting on his part of having actually been pretty good at the game—he agreed to don the pads again, and a much larger pair of creams (Horsburgh was seldom neat, but never so common as to wear plain whites) and have a hit with the NOBs.

Test cricketers must feel (personal resentments aside) that any one of the first six walking out to bat might well make a hundred. I've never played with anyone like that, but Horsburgh was one of the very few where you wouldn't be caught by surprise if it did happen.

Not all of our opponents rated him quite so highly, and as he took the crease on one occasion amidst the usual 'Let's have another'—'We've got them on the run'—'Talk it up 'Towners—this ain't no turkey shoot!'—was a voice crying, 'He's only got one shot.' The first ball Horsburgh stroked loftily over midwicket for six, and turning towards the now less voluble fielder, remarked, 'And that's it.'

He also bowled a cunning leg break, so it was fortunate for the club that he joined us just after I ceased to be captain. As the resident trundler of over-the-wrist stuff I could never have tolerated competition of that order, so he would never have got a bowl. We did once or twice combine in a semi-effective twin spin attack, my bowling being a useful foil to his in that it encouraged a belief that every ball could be hit for four or six—a tenable proposition from my end, but much more risky during Horsburgh's overs.

Peter Horsburgh was an exception to our normal recruiting skills. More typical was the occasion when, one late winter Friday, Pat O'Connor, then Club Secretary, enthusiastically told those of us who'd turned up for off-season training that we were in for a good year: he had just pulled off a recruiting coup by signing up three West Indian fast bowlers who had taken to drinking in Naughton's. This was the era where cricket at a somewhat higher level than ours was dominated by Andy Roberts, Joel Garner, Colin Croft, Malcolm Marshall and the like. Pat relished the thought of NOBs becoming the scourge of Northern Churches D Grade. He wasn't sure if they were any good, but that was beside the point. In his estimation of things all that was necessary was to be big and black and measure out a very long run. The rest would look after itself.

On closer enquiry of the three new prospects themselves, it turned out that one was from Uganda and two from New Guinea, and none of them had ever played cricket in his life. In the event they played not a single game between them, so the psychological effect of Pat's plan was never put to the test.

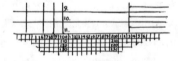

Around this time we did introduce an element of terror into our attack, though it was not so carefully planned as Pat's endeavour. We picked up Dave Mahoney, a big raw-boned ruckman of a size to intimidate the fainter-hearted of our opponents. Dave's athletic abilities had not really been harnessed to cricket. He took the long run so highly recommended by Pat and could work up a reasonable head of steam, but he had no idea at all about length and direction.

Dave was a man entirely without malice, and the beamers he let go were wholly unpremeditated. They were sufficiently frequent, however, to provoke justified complaints from the batsman and arouse a nearly equal degree of alarm in the wicketkeeper.

In his enthusiasm for a game that was not at all his own, Dave was an example of what keeps park cricket going. Most teams rely on an infusion of off-season footballers.

History records that Wills and Harrison devised Australian Rules as a means of keeping cricketers fit over winter, but today the debt goes the other way. If someone in the team plays footy, that means he has a few mates who enjoy competitive sport and are at loose end of a Saturday afternoon in summer, so you're well on the way to rounding out the required eleven. The fact that they actually like running around and are blessed with a certain degree of athleticism is a positive boon for the gentlemen who have arrived at a stage in life where the strenuous exertions demanded while fielding are in conflict with the desire to preserve personal dignity.

NOBs even acquired one genuine star, although his sporting reputation will not benefit from exposure of the relationship. When he first played for NOBs, Jimmy Wynd, long-time friend and former team mate of Steve Loney and Ian Ewing, was running around with the Essendon Twos. But shortly thereafter he was sold off in order to acquire a couple of ageing prima donnas (the eternally inseparable Mike Richardson and Geoff Raines) and Jimmy began to carve out a name for himself at Fitzroy. He was the sort of footballer everyone in Melbourne liked, whatever team they barracked for, a gritty little battler who always gave full value. He won Fitzroy's best and fairest, and usually polled well in the Brownlow. An eternal memory is of Jimmy laying the perfect tackle in the back pocket over at Football Park in Adelaide, only to be penalised for a push in the back, a gimme goal for the Crows. This was the first of a series of seven free kicks in two minutes—three of them totally inexplicable—that gave Adelaide two goals and a kick after the siren to win by a point. Somehow, that was Fitzroy all over.

Jimmy was a footballer first, and a cricketer only in the back yard. His first game for NOBs was the first time he'd ever scored more than twenty. A lot more in fact. After a very sedate start he began knocking the ball around the park, often in the air not far from groping fieldsmen. He began to get distinctly up the nose of an irritable opposition, who put the ball around his ears quite a bit, and he'd snick it over the keeper's head for four.

Two overs to go and he was on 90, but somehow he just couldn't get the strike, or when he did he'd score a single. There are no scoreboards in park cricket, so the batsman doesn't know how many he's got, unless like me he counts them all and never gets enough to lose track. One ball left in the afternoon and he's 94, and at the bowler's end. As if providentially—it certainly wasn't deliberate—a no ball was bowled, from which the batsman managed to score a single. So Jimmy did have one more chance, a bouncer predictably, and proceeded to whack it over fine leg for six, to great exultation from the sidelines and the total demoralisation of the opposition.

But Jimmy's forte was in the field. Nothing could get past him, and anything lifted off the ground was out. The last time the present writer managed to fluke five wickets in a innings with the slowest leg breaks ever to reach the other end of the pitch, most of the credit was due to Jimmy. As I watched the ball disappear at speed over my head I comforted myself with the knowledge that Jimmy was out at long on, and if it wasn't six, he'd catch it. Three times in the afternoon was enough to bring me ridiculously flattering figures.

Taking catches off my bowling is what footy coaches refer to as 'getting the hard ball'.

Max Radcliffe's rugby mates were decidedly less speedy in the field, but did add a great deal of physical bulk to the team profile, which could have an agreeably deterrent effect on the more aggressive of our opponents.

One such was Tom Doolan. It was clear from his general gait that twinkling footwork was not going to be the hallmark of Tom's batting, but no one was quite prepared for the stoic fortitude with which he faced his first ball for the club. He crouched low over the bat, eyes firmly on the bowler, in a stance that could generously be called open—so much so that it resembled the proverbial barn door. He showed no sign of alarm when the ball was pitched short and reared towards the ribs. It would appear that his father had not coached him in the backyard about lifting the bat before the bowler lets go of the ball, as the bat remained fixed in the blockhole. The bowler was not the fastest in the competition, but quite brisk enough to inflict severe pain on an unprotected rib cage. The ball struck square on, with sufficient force to rebound several yards down the pitch. Yet not only did Tom deny the bowler the pleasure of seeing his victim rub the wounded area, he remained rooted in his original stance, as if still waiting for the bowler to deliver the ball.

Bowler, fieldsmen, umpires, and watchers from the boundary were so dumbfounded by the event that no one knew quite what to do. All stood motionless. So did Tom. The game eventually resumed with the puzzled bowler sending down a couple more at a markedly reduced pace. Such imperturbability can have a chastening effect.

It could be inferred from this beginning that Tom's stay at the crease would not be a very productive one, and so it proved to be. Max offered two explanations for this remarkable performance— that Tom was a front-row forward, and that he was a New Zealander. The truth must be in there somewhere.

Another front rower who joined NOBs about the same time was 'Jerker' McCaffery, a splendid team man and a vet, who alas left our company for the more lucrative practice of putting down broken-down jumps horses at the Moonee Valley races on Saturday afternoons.

It would be impertinent to speculate on the origins of Jerker's nickname, but I can vouch for the fact that it was not related to cricket. What used to be (when I kept up with such things) Law 26 of the game used to state that the ball must be bowled, not thrown or jerked. One striking feature of Jerker's cricket was that he could not throw at all. If ever invited to bowl he had to do so in accordance with the law, since his best throws would not have reached the other end of the pitch.

Early in his first game, the ball was played away down to Jerker at deep backward square. To the batsman it appeared there was an easy single and the chance of a second on the throw. Jerker made good ground to the ball and had it in hand as the batsmen turned and took a couple of tentative paces, sizing up the chances of two. They decided not to risk it, as Jerker stood there forty or fifty yards from the pitch with a look in his eye as if to say 'Just you try it, sport!'

The batsmen returned to their creases, but instead of lobbing it in to the keeper Jerker began to walk purposefully towards the stumps tossing the ball up and down in his hand as if it were laden with menace. He had advanced perhaps thirty yards and was level with the square leg umpire when he made an effort to throw the ball in. Despite an orgasmic heave of the body, his throw barely made it half way to the keeper. Various NOBs fell around laughing, and the batting side quickly and accurately assessed the state of play as being always one to Jerker and two more for the throw.

Jerker's fellow prop forward for the Melbourne University rugby club was a chap named Dave Brown, also destined to carve out a modest career for the NOBs. Together they formed two-thirds of the front row known throughout the competition as 'the thin blue line'. Their less than redoubtable half-back, Max Radcliffe, recalls the frisson of genuine terror at the thought that Jerker and Dave were all that stood between him and the marauding menace of the opposing pack.

Dave was a Yorkshireman, consumed like all Tykes of that era with unbounded admiration for Geoff Boycott (invariably referred to as 'Sir Geoffrey'). They spoke with the same accent, and both opened the batting, but the resemblance went further even than that. Both showed the same sense of proportion in balancing the sometimes conflicting demands of team performance and individual achievement. On the day (the author's first game for the club) when Dave topped the score with a personal tally of 6, the general and total humiliation of the team could not diminish Dave's satisfaction in his small personal triumph. It was probably a disappointment to him that none of us managed to get the ball far enough from the wicket for him to run anyone out.

In other facets, the comparison could not be pursued. Dave's program of preparation for the game did not match the dedicated concentration for which Boycott was famous. Though he usually left the pub quite early of a Friday evening, such apparent self-denial was in fact part of a peculiarly English ritual — the Friday night curry. Poms are not famed for the subtlety of their tastes — the hotter the better is the rule of thumb, and Dave's curries frequently left him faint and tottering by start of play. He was much given to describing in detail the sensations of his Saturday morning visit to the lav, which he referred to as 'Rendang's Revenge.'

The residual aroma of the previous night's curry made third man a logical fielding position for Dave— out on his own, removed from the close proximity of the slips. Fielding in the deep added an extra joy to those of us who watched Dave's cricket, since his running action could only be likened to someone wearing a very tight skirt. The ball frequently got past him, but we always enjoyed the sight.

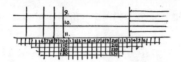

A trickle of footballers kept us more or less up to a quorum in the field, supplemented, as is the habit of park cricket teams, by young kids from the neighbourhood who can fill in as subs in emergencies. In the club's early days the young Keir Strahan, son of Number One Ticketholder Frank Strahan, who lived over the road from the ground, was judged too small and vulnerable for fielding duties, but by the club's final season was a regular and valuable member of the team, belting runs at a great rate and a real tiger in the field.

On another occasion one of the team retired with a broken finger, and Mick Butera's son, the 10-year-old Adrian, formed part of the first and only father–son combination in NOBs history. There was a sensible competition rule that any substitute fieldsman under the age of 14 was not allowed to field closer than twenty yards from the bat. We left young Adrian, for alternate overs, on the third man and long on boundary so he didn't have to move and suggested to him that if there was anything coming that was slow enough for him to feel happy about getting close to it, he was welcome to pick it up and throw it towards the rest of us. Long grass in the outfield and a gen-erous uphill slope towards him lessened the danger to some extent.

Adrian's presence, however diminutive, must have saved us at least a run or two in the afternoon, which was a big improvement on his previous contributions to our performance. When Mick began to be a regular member of the team, it became the practice for Legs Latta to pick him up on his way to the ground. The two-year-old Adrian quickly associated Legs's arrival with Dad disappearing for the rest of the day. Whatever the social circumstances, as soon as Adrian caught sight of Legs there was an outpouring of wailing and grief. So despite the endless affability of his nature, Legs found himself for some years on the outer as a dinner party guest in the Butera household.

But time brings great changes, and if we'd survived for just a few more seasons the now strapping Adrian might have been a handy member of our side. But by this time the thinness of our recruiting base had begun to show through. We did manage to stagger into a second generation of players, and only one person, Max Radcliffe, played in every season of the club's existence, but NOBs never really looked like a long-term proposition. Confining our recruiting to the habitués of the public bar of Naughton's Hotel left us light-on for talent, and for numbers once you discounted those terminally ravaged by the grog and those of an eligible age but unlikely to make it out of bed before start of play next day.

Perhaps a sign of coming oblivion was when Noddy, an unmistakable identity of the public bar, began to be an irregular member of the team. (Nothing that Noddy ever did could be described as 'regular'.) His nickname arose from a quite remarkable facial resemblance to the Enid Blyton figure, and was so ingrained that it came as something of a shock to discover that he had another name of more ordinary formation—well, not quite ordinary, since his parents had chosen to christen him 'Ronan'. Arguably, Noddy could be said to have been a ring-in every time he played, since he never appeared in the scorebook under the name by which he was universally known.

Noddy greeted everyone he knew as they entered the bar with the exclamation, 'Ahhhh, Wombat!'—an Australian witticism of vulgar derivation which particularly appealed to his sense of humour.

One story told by Noddy himself (the only other person in a position to tell certainly wasn't talking) sums up certain elements of his nature, which could prove to be a liability. Noddy ran the newsagency a few doors up from Naughton's and lived above the shop. It must have taken great clumsiness to break through Noddy's torpor, but he awoke one night to hear the unmistakable noises of a burglar downstairs. The intruder was equally aware of the presence upstairs, and called out in a menacing voice, 'Get under the bed and stay there.'

On his own report, Noddy was quite happy to comply with this arrangement, since he had half a dozen cans under the bed and stayed there till he'd finished them. By this time the danger was well past and the appropriate authorities could be notified.

The occasion when he made his debut for NOBs in a competition match was also marked by such fearless attention to duty. It was the only game (fortunately for us) we ever played against a mob who called themselves the Preston Baseballers, and took place in the 1981–82 season. I did not play in this game, but I did the scoring and thus saw the full disaster from reasonably close quarters.

The Baseballers won the toss and batted on a hot dry February day. Clem Simonetto's first ball was slightly wide of off stump, and steered gently to the right of gully. The striker called for a quick single, turned to look for two and was more than pleased to see the ball scooting over the boundary.

The same thing happened with the second ball. As I recorded the score in my book I heard one of the padded-up opposition murmur to his colleagues, 'I think there's a few runs out there today.' Indeed there were—and more to spare. The score mounted dizzily, with NOBs looking less and less determined as the overs passed. Even so, it was quite early in the piece—long before the faintest heart should have thrown in the towel—that the classic moment emerged.

The ball was pushed defensively, but wide enough of cover point to suggest a run. It was clearly an error of tactics by the captain, Steve Loney, to have the lumbering Clem fielding in a key position — but then everyone has to field somewhere. The batsman called for a quick single, and my fellow scorer (less accustomed than I was to watching NOBs in the field) marked down a single against the batsman, one on the bowler's analysis, and ticked one more on the total.

I was not so hasty.

As the batsmen finished the run, they looked across to where Clem was still in pursuit of the ball, and clearly not likely to catch up with it for another few galumphing strides.

Yes? No? Come on! and in fact no danger at all. My companion, with some irritation at having to mess up his scorebook, changed his ones to twos against batsman and bowler and ticked one more on to the total.

I continued to watch.

The second run was comfortably completed by the time Clem picked up the ball and tossed it to the bowler, no more than thirty yards from him. In his exasperation, he threw the ball a bit too hard, and his return passed well over the head of the intended recipient. By good fortune, Noddy was standing in the perfect backing-up position, but not actually watching the game. (There was a female cyclist doing a circuit of Prince's Park at the time.)

Clem's overthrow struck him sharply on the shin and ran away some yards. The more alert of the batsmen called his partner through again. My fellow scorer then converted his twos into threes, as Noddy picked up the ball. Noddy's throw went well wide of the bowler, and also of Clem on the far side of the pitch. Off they went for the fourth, all run from a gentle push to cover. At this point I think the umpire must have called 'over' to bring the sorry farce to an end, allowing me to make a single neat entry in my book.

It was plain to all that Noddy could hold his head up (if that is the appropriate term) only at the most bibulous level of social cricket. Picking him in the main team, as happened several times over three or four seasons, was a desperate expedient.

Undeniably he represented a nadir in recruiting efforts. Optimists maintain that when you're at the bottom the only way is up, but they're wrong. The more likely alternative is out the back door—and that, eventually, is where we went.

4

The Breakout

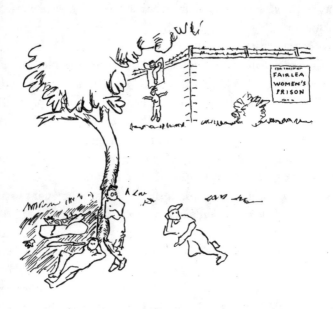

On one occasion, and one only, did NOBs cricket team participate in a significant event, one that mattered to people other than the twenty two players personally involved. 'Participate' is too strong a word — 'observe' would be more accurate. But we did observe from closer range than anyone else, and it was an event that in its own way rippled through public consciousness for quite some time.

On a blazing summer Saturday, the sixth day of February 1982, we played Fairfield Salvation Army on a patch of ground in a very pleasant corner of Yarra Bend Park. To the west, just backward of point, the park sloped down to the river, while an especially vigorous swipe over midwicket, aided by a favourable bounce off Yarra Bend Road, would come to rest against the outer wall of the Fairlea Women's Prison. It was the prison that became the main focus of interest as the afternoon went on.

We won the toss and batted, which means most of the team settling down, in varying degrees of somnolence or nervousness, on a shaded section of the boundary while the opening batsmen go out for brief encounters of the umpteenth kind.

After about an hour's play (not doing too badly by NOBs' standards either) Mick Butera, whose attention had unaccountably strayed from the fierce contest taking place before us, said, 'Have a look what's happening over there.'

What was happening was a denim jacket being thrown from within the walls to land across the razor wire, and one after another several of the residents crawling across it. They jumped in turn the fifteen feet or so to the ground, some of them quite shaken by the fall and bloodied from the wire, and stood in a group not knowing what to do next. As dramatic events go, it was all very much in slow motion.

Had these scenes taken place in Coburg rather than Fairfield, our reactions would certainly have been very different—H Division, Ronald Ryan, the grave of Ned Kelly and other stories of grim moment being part of Melbourne folk lore. Even though it has closed as a prison, the bluestone walls of Pentridge still exhale a palpable aura of desperation and violence.

The jail break we were witness to was altogether less intimidating. The escapees seemed such a sad, bedraggled and bewildered lot that you couldn't help feeling sorry for them. Above all there was no menace, no threat of danger.

After five minutes or so of talking among themselves, some of the group came over to where we were sitting and asked for a lift to the main road—'It's only a mile or two', pointing in the opposite direction to Heidelberg Road, only a few hundred yards away.

Sympathy is one thing; aiding and abetting a felony is another. None of us was forthcoming. I replied with complete honesty, 'I don't have a car.' Biddo said, 'I'm scoring.' Pat O'Connor said, 'I've got to bat soon.'

In post-match voting, Pat's effort was the unanimous choice, on the grounds that it was the only occasion on which anyone, including Pat himself, ever considered his batting to be an excuse for anything at all.

Discouraged by our lack of co-operation, the girls retired to the far side of the ground—carefully observing the proprieties by not straying inside the boundary flags—and sat down on the river bank for a smoke and a dispirited think about things.

Before the enlistment of a research fellow in the School of Laws (see Damien Byers below), and in the absence on that occasion of the Club Philosopher (see Dr Barry Taylor *passim*), we were light on for guidance in the realm of moral philosophy. 'What the hell do we do about that?' was around about the depth of our enquiry into existential possibilities.

On the toss of a coin (the Club Philosopher was not asked for a later ruling on this process of decision-making since it is clearly covered by the Laws of Cricket) it was decided we should report the event to the seemingly oblivious authorities. One of our number— obviously not me, or Biddo, or Pat (though if he had had time to go in to bat he had certainly had enough time to get out)—drove round to the main gate to do a citizen's duty.

In response to much pushing of buzzers and banging on doors, an irate guard appeared wanting to know 'What the bloody hell you bastards think is going on?'

Our delegate responded with appropriate civility by telling them that he had intended to report they'd lost half their inmates but since they weren't interested they should go and get staffed. (In view of the fact that he went on to become one of Victoria's leading Public

Servants, this seems certainly to be the correct reading of the words he is reputed to have uttered.)

Alerted by our warning, the services delegated to protect us innocent citizenry from desperate criminals sprang into action. Not less than half an hour after our warning—time enough perhaps for a head count within the walls—one Holden station wagon carrying two prison officers (wearing caps, so it was very official) screamed its tyres around the bend behind us, leaving the aroma of burning rubber as they sped off much too fast to see that the girls were still sitting near the river, in full view, about sixty or seventy yards from the road.

If the girls lacked clear direction, much more did the warders. A few minutes later they returned slowly, with the beaten air of men who know too well the bureaucratic torture in front of them. As a schoolteacher I rapidly learned the fundamental lesson of service: it's OK as long as they don't break the windows. If there is broken glass there are forms to be filled in and questions to answer. Short of that, you can get away with almost anything. I imagine that a prison breakout is all this and more, with belligerent police thrown in.

I do not recall if someone pointed—perhaps the warders saw for themselves—the huddled group under the gum trees. Since they had no idea where to start looking, this result was as unexpected as it was undeserved, so it was with visible relief that they apprehended the unprotesting fugitives.

Getting them back inside, however, was more of a problem. The shape and size of the Holden station wagon suggest that two in the front (and the officers still wore their caps so dignity required they sit there), two in the back, and two stashed in the storage area, without regard to seatbelt regulations, is about it. That left two over.

We were close enough to hear or deduce most of what was going on while they loaded their four felons into the van. The rest they told to wait until they got back. This showed an admirable trust in human nature, though I doubt the procedure was laid down in the warders' manual.

It took maybe twenty minutes to re-incarcerate the four they had caught—about two hundred yards from the main gate—and come back for the second instalment, which of course was no longer waiting for them. This time they thought to come over to us, the only observers of the whole affair. We were able to tell them, 'They've gone'—as indeed they had, through the grounds of the Fairfield Infectious Diseases Hospital—an institution which, perhaps in the interest of preventing such lawlessness, a rationalising state government subsequently closed down.

The prison officers accepted this news with the air of men who knew the weight of the yoke upon their necks. After one more reckless sortie towards Heidelberg Road they returned to their melancholy duty of reporting the escape to the police.

We're past the tea break in the cricket by now—well after 4 p.m. and the NOBs still knocking up the runs, though none as yet to Patrick. At last the Police made an appearance, first a couple of divvy vans driving south then north again along Yarra Bend Road, and up and down a few more times for good measure.

Later came the boys with the sniffer dogs doing almost the complete perimeter of the gaol, but for some inexplicable reason taking their dogs off to nose around in piles of leaves forty or fifty yards from the point at which the denim jacket, still draped across the wire, stood out like a flag, announcing exactly where the escapees had hit the ground. None of these dedicated enquirers thought to approach the cricket ground and ask if anyone had seen anything until quite late in the piece.

Eventually a car pulled up near our huddle and asked if we knew where they'd gone. Someone volunteered the information that to start off with they'd gone down towards the river. It was a stinking hot summer's day and the cop showed no desire to visit the scene of the crime. He said, 'Don't think we're going down there on a day like this. We've just got air-conditioning in our squad cars—almost had to go on strike for it. If they aren't walking along the road we won't find them.'

The girls must have been some distance away by this time, so the police in their turn decided to call in the media. What this meant was the Channel 7 helicopter swaying to and fro over the outfield at an alarmingly low altitude. Had any of the escaped convicts tried to double up as a fifth slip or an extra fine leg, Channel 7 was ideally placed to notify the police and televise the capture. As it was they simply caused consternation to all of us who had legitimate business there.

Disregarding the decorum of police, prison officers, indeed the escapees themselves, the journos of Channel 7 did not scruple to intrude on the solemn rituals of the sacred game, and play was suspended well before its scheduled close to cope with their demands. They were most anxious for eyewitness accounts of the day's derring-do. None of the NOBs was prepared to make his television debut on such an occasion. One of the opposition, however, saw his chance. Eric—the same Eric who would later endear himself to us by trying to claim a forfeit against us [1]—was an eager interviewee, though as a member of the fielding team with his back to it all for half the time

---

1   Eric was one opponent who carved out a modest place for himself in NOBs folklore. Having once stolen our story and then claimed a forfeit, he later distinguished himself by taking the catch that robbed Max Radcliffe of what would have been the only century of Max's career. On 96, Max hit the ball high into the outfield, confident of at least two on the dropped catch, perhaps the climactic boundary if it rolled on far enough. Eric had never been observed by us to catch anything, or make even a half-decent stop, but on this occasion he made no mistake. It added enormously to the piquancy of the occasion.

and his eyes on other duties he knew almost nothing about what had gone on, except for the conversations that had taken place during the tea break.

It was decided, with the agreement of the opposition, to suspend our much-interrupted play before the scheduled time for stumps so that we could digest the excitement of events and get to the pub early to watch the six o'clock news. By the time we got back to Naughton's the story had grown and changed mightily in everyone's minds, and all were looking forward to the evening news bulletin when we could expect to see Eric's version of events.

The news story was accompanied by aerial film showing Fairlea Prison and the Hospital, which could have been any day of the year but was thought to be a record of events only because it had been taken on that particular day. Even though shot from the helicopter which had terrorised us, it failed to show the gallant deeds of the white clad gentlemen below, which would have truly established it as being a record of the precise occasion. The commentary was especially approved, containing the maximum number of inaccurate clichés— 'Within minutes the area was buzzing with police . . .' and so on.

Opinion was divided on whether Eric's testimony would match his fielding ability. He did not disappoint. Not a single fact was correct. But the feature all appreciated was that the only NOB to be seen was Max Radcliffe, standing in the background, rather stiffly posed in front of the little red Renault he used to drive. When asked about this cameo role he said, 'Those girls looked like they might have some fairly tough boy friends, and I didn't want any of them knowing my registration number.'

Two of the girls avoided capture for quite some weeks, and that part of the story sputtered along in the newspapers. But the day's events had much sadder consequences within the gaol. The prison staff, who had already so dashingly demonstrated their efficiency to us, decided that the best way of coping with the bolted horse was to shut the stable door, so all inmates were locked in their cells.

How a prison population reacts to such treatment, especially when wrought to a pitch, as at a major breakout, is well enough documented, and it all happened at Fairlea. There was a riot, some of the inmates started a fire in their wooden dormitory block, which then of course they could not escape, and three died in their cells of smoke inhalation with two more seriously injured and taken to hospital.

We managed to persuade ourselves that nothing we could have done would have changed this part of the story.

But the misfortune of some is the blessing of others. A few months earlier a television soapie called *Prisoner* had struggled into prime time. A Melbourne production, notionally set in a Victorian women's prison, the locale could just about have been mistaken for Fairlea, though of course 'all resemblance to persons . . . etcetera'. For such a program, battling for storylines, the Fairlea breakout was a godsend.

It was not a show I ever watched, but station promos are inescapable. Within a couple of weeks of the actual event, and thereafter for (it seemed) years, there would be a sudden irruption during ad breaks of hatchet faced women glowering or shouting at each other, with a melodramatic voice-over relating to lesbian passions, deeds of violence by and against authority and, unfailingly, death by fire.

All human suffering is grist to the mill. But never once in all the reproduced anguish derived from events of genuine tragedy was there ever a mention—let alone a long panning camera shot—of those who toiled so effortfully outside the walls that day, or of the pain of poor Pat from Halifax, another duck, alas.

5

Satanic influences

At the time of its inception, though the blush of youth had faded from the cheeks of most of the participants, NOBs was almost exclusively a bachelor outfit. Down the years, matrimony and its attendant responsibilities claimed a number of victims, but in those early days the freedom to spend almost unlimited hours in the bar was a necessary precondition for the club coming into existence at all.

Footloose and not overburdened by a puritan conscience, we perhaps succumbed to the temptations of the Devil at least as often as most of our church-going opponents. But it is no part of this book's intention to catalogue the moral defects to which we, individually and collectively, were liable. Rather, the title of this chapter refers to the more recent revelation, courtesy of the former captain of South Africa, that the failure to conduct cricket matches with a ruthless and uncompromised will-to-win is in fact the work of Satan. Aparently cricket is unique among sporting contests in this respect. When suspicions arise in horseracing that results are questionable, less theological explanations are sought. And in motor racing, such conduct seems to be not only approved, but applauded.

The farcical finish of the 1998 Formula One Grand Prix in Melbourne, when by prior arrangement one driver slowed down to allow his team-mate to pass him and win the race, evoked from the governing body of the sport — though only after a mouthful of teeth had been pulled — the immortal phrase, 'conduct prejudicial to competition'. Jockeys are deprived of their livelihood for similar activities, but it took a public outcry for anyone in motor racing to admit there was something a bit whiffy about rigging the result, and those responsible positively refused to say it wouldn't happen again.

Some readers might recall that in the early games of the 1999 cricket World Cup, Hansie Cronje, when captaining in the field, was the pioneer of the electronic earpiece for information on tactics. When ordered to remove it, he was as scornful as only the truly righteous can ever be of those who could not see the way of the future and were resisting the inevitable. Now it seems that the earpiece on the field, the mobile phone in the dressing room and the Indian bookmaker at the end of the satellite are all manifestations of the Devil.

The closest NOBs ever got to electronic gadgetry was Clem Simonetto's transistor radio, permanently glued to the racing channel. Doubtless Clem would have appreciated the hot wire, which would have spared him the indignity of calling out every so often during the afternoon, 'What won the fourth at Moonee Valley?'

Poorly kitted out with the electronics sported by the up-to-the-minute cheat, we also related to bookmakers only in the suppliant role. That is, we gave them money, never the other way round.

And yet it is a sign of how deeply the canker has entered into the soul of Australian cricket that we too must plead guilty when those charged with rooting out corruption get around to us. In this chapter, for the benefit of future commissions of enquiry, names will be named, let the blame fall where it will, and those responsible skewered for their past misdeeds. For results were rigged and matches were thrown.

This was not a common occurrence, but at least two instances will be fully documented, as will a more pervasive lack of the Christian zeal in the pursuit of victory that would have been appropriate in a Church competition and acceptable to players more deeply pious than us. The phrase 'conduct prejudicial to competition' seems expressly designed to serve as an epitaph for NOBs's on-field activities

From all that has been said about NOBs's habitual approach to the game of cricket, it could rightly be inferred that courage in adversity, heroic fightbacks from perilous positions, or digging deep to overcome the pain barrier were not a common feature of our team performances. Once a batting collapse set in, that was it for the day. Team morale seldom lifted us to valiant efforts. No McCosker returned to the crease, broken jaw swathed in bandages, to lift the side's spirit. No Eddie Paynter struggled from his sick bed to take his tottering part in the team effort. (Unless coping with a monumental hangover is a virtue, in which case we were noble strivers.)

Even so, certain episodes in the history of the club show a lack of dedication and fighting spirit that make one wonder why we ever bothered taking the field at all. Perhaps that was our first mistake, given that as soon as we were on it our immediate ambition was to get back off and into the pub as soon as possible. That the entire enterprise was a mistake from start to finish is certainly an arguable proposition.

My first intimation of the wilting performances to which the team was liable came early in my association—the very first time I played, late in the 1979–80 season. Dragooned on Friday night as a result of immoderate boasting and the vaguely expressed notion of having another crack at the game after a long lay-off, I found myself at Prince's Park next day, donning the crumpled whites, checking for moth-holes in the jumper, relieved to have finally located the missing right boot.

It had been a chance meeting the night before with an irregular drinking mate of long standing—none other than Club Founder Patrick O'Connor—that had led to this impasse. Pat wasn't playing in this particular game, but had volunteered to pick me up and take me to the ground. The jangled nerves were partly due to the previous evening's activities, but also to the fact that Pat had completely forgotten about the lift and so, leaving it till the last moment, I had had to make a sprint to get to the ground more or less at starting time.

I probably shouldn't have worried too much, since NOBs were almost never known to start a game on time—especially at home where we were responsible for laying the mats and putting out the flags. The Club Treasurer would calculate the likely fines as the visitors twiddled their thumbs waiting for the ground to be put in a condition for play to start.

Today, like every other, we were slow off the mark—but it wouldn't have done to be too late on this occasion. Our opponents were a fine upstanding group of lads from Regent Baptist, possessing, as an ironic female friend described me in my own Baptist days, a scrubbed air of moral purity. It was all they needed on this occasion.

NOBs won the toss and elected to bat. As an unknown interloper, I was shovelled well down the batting order, Number 8 in fact, and so had time to take in the atmosphere, chat to new team-mates, assess the standard of play. Or would have done so in any normal unfolding of the game.

A wicket in the second over, with still not a run on the board, was a bad start, but far from unknown at any level of the game. Another two in the same over was a premonition of disaster. The main activity in our camp was desperate scrabbling in the kit by the next man in, trying to find a second pad of any kind to go with the one he had half put on, as raucous yells from the middle announced yet another hapless victim.

I cannot claim to have been more composed and dignified than any of my predecessors as I walked out to bat with the score at 6 wickets down for 9 runs. But I was at least aware of how one should approach the task in such circumstances. When I joined my first park cricket team in Sydney (Petersham Baptist, indeed), a much younger and more foolishly ambitious aspirant, I was, week after week, galled by watching six or eight batsmen I judged far inferior to me get themselves out before I was given a dig, with the dregs of total athletic incompetence as my only companions. In my impatience I would fling the bat for a paltry half a dozen before the inevitable skier and humiliated departure.

My grandfather, who had played for the same team fifty years earlier and was wiser in his knowledge of the game, understood my frustration and advised me, 'Just make sure you're not out at the end of every innings. They'll soon give you a bat higher up.'

There is something very true to the spirit of cricket in this advice. With the wholehearted conviction that one is serving the long-term best interests of the team, one can concentrate exclusively on one's personal stakeholding. So a patient three not out became the focus of my efforts, rather than the rapid half dozen, caught at mid on. And indeed it wasn't long before I was opening the innings.

It was clear that a similar tactic was best adapted to the state of the game in my NOBs debut, though three not out seemed quite a size-able total in this particular context.

No great reserves of patience were required to see the innings out, but my thirst for red ink was not to be assuaged. Last man out (caught off a mis-cue into the covers, as I recall), my four was topped only by Dave Brown's 6, which included the only boundary of the innings. However, Legs Latta, coming in last but managing four himself, with the not out as well, must be classed as the second most successful performer—though degrees of achievement are difficult to determine when the scale is so minute.

So it was that NOBs took their turn in the field barely an hour into the game (and the late start was responsible for a good portion of that). Second ball of the first over, and Clem Simonetto scattered the opening batsman's stumps. Momentarily we held the advantage. It had taken more than an over before we had been one down for none! The remaining batsmen, however, were not to be tempted to enter into the spirit of the occasion, and a couple of hefty swipes to the boundary soon altered the position.

As one Radcliffe delivery was despatched with tremendous velocity over the grassless outfield and beyond, Max was heard to request the fieldsman shambling after it, 'Get me a *Sporting Globe* on the way back!' [1]

---

1   In summers long past, the 'pink paper', as the *Globe* was affectionately known, relied on racing for its sales. No one bought it for the cricket. But in winter, it was a marvel. That it could hit the newsagents within an hour of the final siren each Saturday was a miracle of organisation, owing much to the formulaic style that aided rapid summarisation and made every game sound much the same. The grainy photographs, all the more indistinct on their pink background, could have been taken the previous week or five years earlier, so they could be set up well in advance. Even so, before we had replays and games live to air from two thousand kilometres away three days and nights a week, the *Globe* answered the craving of the sporting addict in those innocent days: to sit over a beer and fish and chips and read the magic names of the heroes and imagine games now faded into history.

In much less than three hours Regent Baptist rattled on a couple of hundred for a wicket or two more and declared well before stumps to have another tilt at their tawdry and demoralised opposition.

My grandfather's advice was no less efficacious now than it had been twenty years earlier, for I found myself catapulted from number 8 to second wicket down. Apparently, it had not passed unnoticed by the hierarchy that in my carefully selfish first innings I had been at the crease while the score mounted dizzily from 9 to 27 — so I had seen more runs go on the board than anyone else, despite the modesty of my personal contribution.

By this time I had seen enough of the NOBs to know, when I was told my new batting position, that I'd better start looking for a pair of pads as quickly as possible.

There is a nice story told about the incomparable Sydney Barnes, playing Minor Counties for Staffordshire in his late fifties, when some young colt with the Lancashire Seconds thought he'd like to take a look from behind the bowler's arm at how the great man used to do it. Number six in the batting order, there was plenty of time to wander round the park, but as he headed off his captain told him to get back and put his pads on. As the story goes, 'there were four of us all padded up and waiting. And we were all out in the middle and back again in half an hour.'[2]

There was certainly no Sydney Barnes playing for Regent. On the other hand, there didn't need to be. I was back in action almost as soon as in the first innings, and another went down before stumps, leaving us 3 for 30 at the end of the first day's charades.

This was the occasion when the opposing captain, in an attempt to get the names straight in the score book, came over to find out who the two not out batsmen were, only to find neither of us knew our names.[3]

---

2   See *Wisden* 1968 for Barnes's obituary.

3   For a more complete account, see page 52.

When play resumed on the second Saturday there was an odd aspect to the behaviour of Regent Baptist in the field. Several of their number were most insistent about knocking us over before half past three. The time was quite specific, and the slip-field was abuzz with it. The only other occasion when I had noticed an opposition so focused not just on an early finish (generally it is pub-oriented teams that are so inclined) but on finishing by a particular hour, I later found out that someone was running a book on how soon it would be all wrapped up, and considerable sums of money would change hands on the result.

This seemed out of character for the good Baptists, so it served in some measure to restore my sense of the fitness of things to discover eventually that nothing so sordid as money was involved, but rather that one of their team had an aunt who lived near the ground, and if he could get to the phone by half past three to give her good warning, they were all invited for tea and scones.

It was our contribution to turning them from the narrow paths of righteousness that we were able to keep them out in the field just long enough for them to miss the engagement.

Though we managed to stave them off for slightly longer than the previous Saturday, nothing that could qualify as a fightback took place, and the final margin was an innings and plenty.

On this occasion, as on all others when total humiliation was visited upon us, the team reaction was not one of despondency, but rather of heightened joviality in the bar post-match. As each dismissal was re-lived over copious beers, the inadequacies of one's technique that had allowed it to happen were helpfully and repeatedly pointed out by one's teammates.

A clear gap in talent between the two sides largely explains the way the Regent game went, but it was certainly compounded by a signal lack of application on our part.

This tendency to allow collective attention to stray from the job in hand became even more obvious to me in the next encounter, an away game against a club known as Edinburgh, who derived their name from the Edinburgh Gardens in North Fitzroy where their home ground was located. It is a very pretty ground, in a pleasantly treed park, overlooked by the gracious terraces of Albert Crescent.

Generally our loyalty to Naughton's drew us back to our home bar, even from grounds scattered far over the northern suburbs. By comparison, Edinburgh Gardens was a mere hop away, but on my pointing out that the Homestead Hotel, two blocks from the ground, was now run by the Boscacci boys, former landlords of the Prince Alfred, we decided to make that our destination on the first day of the game.

The Prince Alfred in Grattan Street is another university pub. Almost all the troops had had a few (and more than a few) beers there, and Biddo had even worked behind the jump for a while, so old acquaintances were to be renewed. So hospitable were Garry and Graham, so freely flowed the jugs courtesy of the house that we decided to make the Homestead our jumping off point for next Saturday's efforts.

More than once in this narrative it has been hinted that NOBs were unusual in that not only did we adjourn to the bar after stumps, but a large proportion of the team would meet there beforehand as well. Some restrained themselves to a soda squash, others a necessary hair of the dog, but the Edinburgh game was the only occasion where we scheduled a full blown counter lunch before the start of play. I think we had a full turnout (certainly by the end of lunch), and anyone who intended to keep himself strictly in order before the game would have been hard pressed to do so.

The first day's play had seen Edinburgh knock up a respectable 250 and give us half an hour or so to start the chase. Losing only one wicket was a creditable effort on our part, especially in view of the Regent debacle last time out, and in the face of a young thatch-haired kid who belted the ball down at considerable pace.

As a quarter to two—the official time for the start of play—drew nearer, some of the more responsible team members were heard to mention the cricket match up the road we were supposed to be taking part in. Captain Bernie O'Brien took a sternly disciplinarian approach and sent off not only the two not out batsmen but also one extra to pad up just in case. The rest of the team continued with sherbet dessert.

Such serene confidence has not been seen since the halcyon days when Sussex would leave one man padded up while the rest of the side repaired to the beach at Hove, as Fry and Ranjitsinhji batted on in the sunshine.

In ones and twos, as each jug reached its bottom, a few stragglers would saunter round the boundary to see how the side was getting on. By some stroke of fortune we were never actually short of a man to go in at the fall of a wicket, though sometimes it was, like the battle of Waterloo, a damned fine run thing.

I suppose it can't have been all that long really before the full eleven assembled. It just seemed like it to those of us over-indoctrinated by the propaganda of the game who felt this was not quite the way competitive sport should be undertaken.

The young quickie was regularly knocking over whoever we sent out to face him, and 250 (which would at that time have been a club record score) was obviously out of the question when Pat O'Connor went in to join skipper Bernie O'Brien with seven wickets down.

The fact that Patrick is the most gregarious of men and would have been the most reluctant to leave the bar while drink was still flowing was not the only reason he was listed low in the batting order. To those who have been privileged to see the long succession of ducks Pat has made, what happened that February afternoon still seems beyond belief.

Never one to get his eye in, Pat went bare headed for the bowling from the start. A comprehensive six over mid wicket in the first few balls set the tempo. The young kid was mightily aggrieved, in the manner of all fast bowlers, by such treatment. Had he seen more of Pat's batting, astonishment would have got the upper hand of resentment. The next one was predictably short and fast, and it went the same way as the ball before.

The madder he got the shorter he bowled, and the harder and further Pat seemed to hit them.

At the other end, the captain derived inspiration from Pat's onslaught, and dealt out a few hearty blows of his own. His way of handling the short ball, however, was determined strictly by considerations of self-preservation. When the ball got up around the eyebrows Bernie went straight to ground. For a couple of overs he spent more time on his bum than upright, and when he ran between wickets he was accompanied by a faint halo of red dust shaken from his creams.

Pat too was forced into the odd evasive move in between belting the cover off the ball, but his half century came up in well under the quarter hour. Bernie's wasn't much longer, albeit considerably more dusty. Pat made 55 in no time, before a mishit spelled the end of his quixotic charge. A scoring chart of his innings would have revealed that the ideal field setting was nine men on the midwicket boundary, but even so five hits would have gone right over their heads.

What marked this innings out as an O'Connor classic and the absolute highlight of his career was that not only did Pat play the innings of his life, but we still lost. The brief moment of frenetic glory was not enough to close the gap, and we fell a respectable twenty or so short of the target.

Some who saw the innings were moved to wonder what Pat might do with a clear head and a steady hand. Unfortunately, the club score book gives a consistent and depressing answer to such speculation.

The O'Connor–O'Brien partnership was perhaps the most rousing backs-to-the-wall effort NOBs ever produced, but this particular match earns its place in this chapter by virtue of the pre-game preparation—irresponsible frivolity of a high order in a team taking part in an organised competition.

On some occasions the lack of dedication was not shared universally, but confined to a more local level. The most painful memory retained by the present writer concerns the first semi-final NOBs ever found themselves unexpectedly dropped into.

Making the top four shouldn't have come as too much of a surprise really. The general shrinkage of the competition mentioned elsewhere naturally made itself felt at the lowest levels—that is to say, our level. At the start of a season the fixture list would be frequently re-jigged to cater for teams dropping out, or being promoted to higher grades to replace others who failed to get sufficient numbers together.

This particular season, with the schedule being changed every week, we played Thomastown United in three of the first four games, the other being against East Thomastown, which was in its debut season, being a breakaway group of players from an apparently not so United Thomastown. When things settled down three facts seemed fairly clear: firstly, there were only six teams in our grade, D1;[4] secondly, two of them were probably even worse than us; thirdly, we would never have the ghost of a chance of beating East Thomastown.

Accordingly, at the end of the regular season we found ourselves in fourth spot, and therefore drawn to meet top side, East Thomastown, in the semi-final.

We had stood a reasonable chance of escaping the final four, as we had just played East Thomastown in the last home and home

---

4   See page 4 for an explanation this nomenclature.

game and suffered a monumental defeat. The end of our second innings was hastened by a devastating hat trick taken by their fast bowler, universally known as The Beast.

Unfortunately, neither of the sluggardly teams below us was able to pick up enough points to spare us our fate in the game to come.

For reasons that entirely escaped me even at the time—perhaps it was my turn in the shout when the decision happened to be made— I found myself captain of the team for a couple of seasons around this point.

One tactical decision concerning this semi-final still lodges vividly in the mind.

In the days before Shane Warne reminded everyone of the sheer beauty of leg break bowling, every bowler in park cricket just belted it down as fast as they could and hoped for the best. As soon as the flighted ball rose above eye level a collective madness would grip the young blades of the Northern and Combined Churches. Here was money for jam. Like MacDougall, who, 'when he missed, the impetus would spin him three times round', they teed off mightily.

As a purveyor of the slowest trundlers imaginable,[5] I expected to cop several hefty blows but was always confident that, sooner or later, the half volley would drop a foot or so shorter and I knew there'd be enough turn to catch the outside half of the bat for a steepling catch to cover, or past it altogether for an easy stumping while the batsman was still trying to control the centrifugal forces he had set in motion. The full tosses that never got a chance to turn were all useful inducements to keep them swinging from the two-bob seats.

---

5   I always greatly esteemed the opinions of reputedly the greatest of all leg spinners, Bill O'Reilly, in his days as a commentator on the game. He seems to have had my style of leg breaks specifically in mind when he wrote: 'Tossing the ball high should be regarded as an unfailing sign that the bowler is wasting everybody's time, and would be much better off if he turned his attention to batting, or feeding the chooks.' (Bill O'Reilly, *Tiger*, Fontana Collins, Sydney, 1985, p. 211).

I hatched a plan accordingly. Steve Loney and Clem Simonetto were, when all's said and done, our only two bowlers worth the name, and both bowled brisk and tight. East Thomastown's top order, playing carefully, were likely to lose a wicket or two, but survive the new ball reasonably intact, ready to create havoc when the third and fourth stringers came on.

I thought perhaps if we could get one of their better players to throw caution to the winds against my rubbish before he'd really got his eye in we might just grab a wicket for free. On the way to the ground at Mayer Park, I said to Steve, 'Don't be surprised if I come on after only an over or two. If I get wicket I'll come straight off and you'll be back on.'

So at what must have seemed to the batsmen an absurdly early stage of the innings on came the cream puffs. It all went exactly as scripted. The opening batsman lit up like a pinball machine and in my first over aimed a huge blow at the long on boundary without quite getting to the pitch of the ball. Any one of four fieldsmen could have got under it, and fortunately the one who did took the catch.

It was at this precise moment that I lost sight of the overall team plan. 'If one, why not another?' I thought. The second over all sat up outside the leg stump just asking to be helped on the way for a series of fours. I foolishly convinced myself that that was too bad to be true and just one more would put things right.

By the time sanity returned, the batsmen were well away, and Steve had to come back on and try to pick up the pieces.

I was not the only one to fluke a wicket that day. One unfortunate characteristic of Biddo's medium-pace slingers was a tendency (more regular than it should have been) for the ball to become stuck in his hand for an extra fraction of a second, causing the delivery to drop alarmingly short. This particular one landed not far from his big toe and looped lazily almost straight up in the air. He'd got it just far enough along the pitch for it to have some forward momentum, and the stunned batsman watched in amazement as the ball floated twenty or so feet above his head.

He had plenty of time to take stock, and at some point it occurred to him that it might just land on top of the middle stump. There are few shots in the coaching manual to cope with such a delivery, and he decided on the two-handed overhead tennis smash, known in some circles as the 'clobber shot'. But his timing was sadly astray, and he succeeded only in hitting the ball straight back where it had come from. It described an arc at least as high as the first one and ended up right where Biddo was standing, and he obligingly effected the caught-and-bowled.

The batsman was a red-headed kid of fiery temperament who rather fancied himself as a cricketer. As the catch was taken he threw his bat on the ground with a burst of profanity. But whatever his disappointment, he had to pick up his bat and go. As he walked despondently past our amused but sympathetic fieldsmen, Max Radcliffe consoled him with the thought, 'At least you have the satisfaction of knowing you got out to the worst ball ever bowled.' This resulted only in another explosion of profanity, and the bat was despatched clean over the boundary line.

In such a haphazard fashion, we did rather well to get East Thomastown out half way through the second session, their total swollen by the early splurge of runs. But this only served to bring to a head the problem that had been lurking since before the game started: who was going to open the batting against The Beast?

Geoff Crossman and Max Radcliffe had opened for us almost every game, but Crossman wasn't playing. Max seemed to accept the inevitable, but there was no sign of anyone queuing up to join him.

The previous week I had copped a first baller against The Beast, middle man in his hat trick, clean bowled by one I never even saw. But after a forlorn survey of the team it looked as if I was the most expendable item around.

There was no prior discussion about who would face, but as we walked out together to bat, there was a brisk breeze blowing from the north, so it should have been no surprise to me that Max engineered himself to that side. As we approached the middle he veered more and more widely towards the non-striker's end, as if it were the naturally accepted thing that the skipper should have the honour of taking block to start the innings off against The Beast, coming downhill with the wind at his back.

In the first over he put one on a length around the line of off stump. I played forward defensively only to be smacked on the back leg around about an inch and a half from where it really hurts. The next ball looked similar, I played the same shot and got hit in exactly the same spot. Both times I thought I'd picked the line all right, but it's not really fair when someone at that pace can move the ball in the air as well.

Theorists and commentators are forever telling us that the really dangerous delivery is the one that leaves the bat, but this experience forced me to disagree. Class players worry about outside edges—I was more concerned about vital organs.

My discomfiture was not diminished by the howls of obvious glee coming from my team mates at the boundary line, nor by the advice from Max at the other end—all said with a smile of complete enjoyment on his face—'Don't rub it! Don't rub it!' A batsman could be lying poleaxed and all the sympathy he'd get from his partner would be, 'Don't let them think they've hurt you.' The opposition had no doubts at all about what they'd done to me.

It couldn't be said that I defied The Beast for all that long, but it was quite long enough to appreciate the subtleties of Max's way of coping with extreme pace. Several times I managed to work the ball far enough away from the field to contemplate a single, but Max was caution personified. By contrast, when he was facing the more pedestrian new-ball bowler at the other end and tucked one behind point, there was never any doubt he was coming back for a hairs-breadth two.

In all the time I was out there I think Max faced one ball from The Beast, dropped it dead at the crease and took a single of the kind that is usually called cheeky, but on this occasion would be more aptly termed craven hearted.

In the pub after the game, and repeatedly over the years since, not only has there been no hint of shame from Max about this way of conducting the game, it is a particular point of pride for him to recall how skilfully he handled The Beast that day.

There is a story, perhaps apochryphal, about Yorkshire caught on a treacherous wicket, when Len Hutton carried his bat for not very many. After the debacle one of his less talented and heavily battered colleagues was bemoaning what fate had dished out. The only sympathy he got from Hutton was the piece of advice that in such conditions the good batsman is the one up the other end.

Turning over the strike and shielding your colleagues had no part in Max's game plan on this occasion. And sure enough he was the one not out at stumps. Next Saturday, with The Beast refreshed and pawing the ground again, it rained, and no play was possible. Virtue may be its own reward, but the lack of it is very useful at times too.

Self-preservation is not only understandable; once one has got past the ridiculous nonsense that has been spawned about the uniquely noble, character-forming qualities of cricket, one can see that it is close to the heart of this most endearingly selfish of games, so Max had the oldest traditions of cricket with him when he boasted of his achievement.

However, it is hard to pretend that virtual abandonment of a match can be defended on any grounds at all. Following the semi-final, I was able to conceal the Mark of the Beast (inflicted, appropriately, with a six-stitcher), engraved as it was not on the brow but on the inner thigh, but the Sign of Satan himself was clearly visible on those who played in the next couple of seasons when the captaincy slipped from my grasp.

Come the last round of the 1983–84 season, NOBs had ceased to be even what is called a mathematical possibility for the finals, but there were two teams still locked in contention for fourth spot. One of these was West Lalor, our opponents in our last game, and by co-incidence their rivals were playing on a closely adjacent ground, just a few hundred yards away across Prince's Park.

After several seasons now West Lalor and NOBs were old sparring partners, and on pretty good terms with each other, considering the aggro so many clubs poured into their Saturday afternoons.

The team we played against was the second XI for a side competing at a more lofty level, and was part of a complex community sporting organisation, running to football teams in winter, basketball, netball, darts, and for all we knew mid-week bingo for the oldies—as against NOBs, a rag-tag bunch scraped together on Friday evenings. They always seemed to have a greater depth of resources, but for one reason or another we had a handsome advantage on the win/loss record.

Well into the second day of the game it was as certain as such things can be that another feather was to be added to the cap. Our 200 was not an insuperable target, but wickets were falling on schedule before tea.

During the break there was some discussion amongst the leadership of how the rest of the day might go. The chief worry was not getting West Lalor out, but whether they would agree to call the game off at the end of their innings and join us for an early start in the pub. What complicated matters was that the governing body who presided over our competition had long been anxious to prevent teams agreeing to an early finish after one innings each. They were firm believers in the principle that if you don't like it, it must be doing you good, and that the moral benefits of sporting competition were greatly increased by both teams staying out there for the extra half hour or so while a meaningless 2 for 37 was entered on a brand new page of the score book and a few fresh skin lesions were exposed to the fierce western sun. It also gave the donkeys who would never otherwise get a bowl a chance to roll their arm over and add to the none for 25 taken off them the last time they'd been given an over.

The ingenious method employed by the competition to induce us to act against all sense and reason was to award bonus points for second innings scores as well as first innings. Actually winning the game was still the best way to scoot up the ladder, but the minute fractions of decimal points accumulated over a season of doggedly batting on until six o'clock could be significant in a tight battle for fourth place—as was now the case.

West Lalor had a regular tic-tac going to keep up with the progress of the game over the other side of Prince's Park. It seemed that a first innings win would see them home and safe, but if they lost they'd need to scrape together all the loose change they could.

When play resumed after tea, Ian Ewing gravely compounded the problem by putting in a more effective bowling spell than we were used to seeing. In about ten overs up to drinks he conceded six runs and, on top of the three wickets he took, was beating the bat at least twice an over. Runs had completely dried up and there were only two bunnies left to ferret out.

Carefully assessing the state of the game—and of the game over the other side of the park—captain Steve Loney informed his best mate, 'I think your groin's about to go.' First up after drinks and our match winner is on his haunches, barely able to complete the over before staggering to first slip to see the game out.

Steve himself had bowled well earlier in the day, but his reserves of stamina had clearly given out and he was unable to return to the bowling crease, so Shane Ryan took over the attack. A no ball which skittled the stumps and a snick just wide of the keeper suggested that Shane was not the bowler who best suited the team's unusual needs. Don't use a stopgap when a floodgate is required.

Eventually a pair of bowlers, Rob Irwin and Legs Latta, was found whose best endeavours could not quite stop West Lalor passing our score. It is important to point out, in the team's defence, that those who bowled did so as well as they could—it was just that those who might have done better were temporarily rested.

What happened next was entirely predictable. The ingenuity required to coax twenty or so runs out of the tail was nothing compared to the nuisance of getting them out when enough was enough.

We'd already used up most of the time we'd promised ourselves in the pub by the time the innings ended. And now the news from the other side of Prince's Park was more dire. Perhaps West Lalor could still miss the finals. Their captain, known to us as the Turk (though presumably the scorebook had a different designation), was under pressure. His natural inclinations were for a beer with us at Naughton's, but the team's arithmetic said 'Play on!'

We stood by, well within earshot, as the Turk and his players caucused. 'But we could still miss out,' was a plaint we heard voiced more than once. Ian Ewing took it upon himself to interpose one comment into their deliberations. The broad structure of his statement was, 'We gave you first innings points. How many more do you want?' The reader may care to interpolate obscenities at will into the above utterance, but would find it difficult to match the colour and degree of emphasis contained in the original.

This seemed to tip the balance in our favour, and both teams headed for Naughton's, still a couple of pots' worth before official time for stumps.

Though it was the duty of the home team to ring through close of play scores to the Association secretary, the Turk undertook to perform the task on our behalf, since he wanted to find out what had happened in the other games.

No mobile phones in those days—you had to wait your turn at the phone box outside. Some time later the Turk returned to the bar ashen faced. The final calculations had put them out of the finals by about as many hundredths of a point as corresponded to taking one of our wickets in the second innings.

Though we had nothing at all going for the other team, whoever they were, we were in a much better position than the Turk to appreciate the comic aspects of the situation.

Undoubtedly, throwing a game is the ultimate disgrace. But, having coped with so many intermediate disgraces, some of us find that, in the perspective of years, irony lends a certain charm even to our unforgivable misdeeds.

Earlier in this chapter it was asserted there were two matches where NOBs shamefully gave the whole thing away. But since the second occasion was a Grand Final it deserves, with circumstantial detail, a chapter to itself.

6

The Royal Oak

The summer of 1982–83 was very nearly our season of destiny. That is, if you define destiny as an entry in 6-point nonpareil in the most inaccessible sporting page of Monday's *Age*.

For most of the cricket season, column after column tabulates the scores phoned in from descending grades in more and more obscure competitions. A line must be drawn somewhere, and that somewhere is normally several rungs above where NOBs competed. Come the start of the finals in late February, first half, then three-quarters of these games disappear, but according to an adaptation of Parkinson's Law that dictates that there will always be enough news to fill every page of the paper, more and more matches worthy of notice are discovered, until even teams like NOBs are thrust into pallid limelight.

Distribution statistics are not sensitive enough to show the small blip in circulation that surely must occur when the reading public is given the chance to follow the progress of such contests.

But NOBs did make the Grand Final in March of 1983, and thus became part of the public record. It was the only Grand Final in which we participated, although two seasons later we came as close as maybe, when Mick Cushen dropped a catch in the semi-final with 9 wickets down and the opposition 4 runs short. Later opinion was divided between those (viz. Mick himself) who maintained it was a heroic effort even to get to the ball, and others (everyone else in the team) who said it was an absolute sitter. Several of those present were able to make comparisons with a similar incident a year or so earlier, where a mark as the siren sounded gave Ian Ewing a kick at goal that could have won the VFA Second Division Reserves Grand Final for Northcote. By Ian's account it was a towering torpedo that just fell short of the massive distance required; everyone else thought he must have stubbed his toe.

The 1982–83 season began promisingly for NOBs with an outright win (very rare for us) over St Mary's. In hindsight there may have been a straw in the wind here for the future of the Association. Pub teams are one thing, but once you let the Catholics in, who knows where it might end?[1]

But the second game gave us a more sobering taste of the season's realities, for we were drawn to play a team calling itself The Royal

---

1   In the late sixties the South Suburban Churches Cricket Association would annually debate and defer a motion to drop the word 'Protestant' from the clause governing clubs eligible to compete—not that anyone contemplated letting the Micks in, but the semblance of ecumenism was very fashionable back then. After one AGM our club delegate was able to report that discussion had followed a predictable course until a Sri Lankan delegate had addressed a question to the Chairman: 'This word Protestant—what she mean?' That seemed a nice way of putting 400 years of European history into perspective.

Oak. The first day of the game panned out pretty well for us. It was Caulfield Cup Day, and the rain poured down from early morning. We hoped we might catch our opponents at their home bar to call off play for the day, but the barman of The Royal Oak in Nicholson Street Fitzroy had never heard of a cricket team connected to the pub. We were later to learn that this mob based themselves on another establishment of the same name in a closely adjoining suburb.

Having missed them on the phone, a quorum had to head off to their home ground in Royal Park to solemnly consult their representatives and formally agree to the obvious—that no play was possible that day. This gave us a full afternoon in the bar with the form guide and the chance for Horsburgh and Radcliffe to take surplus cash off anyone foolish enough to enter the sweeps they arranged.

The second Saturday, no such relief was granted us, and a one-day game, 40 overs a side, took place with The Royal Oak easy victors. One fact that was soon apparent was that their opening bowler was some degrees better than we were used to facing. While one can make a fairly swift assessment of the quality of the opposition bowling (taking into account such factors as how hard you need to rub the bruised thigh), judging their batting is a little more subjective, since they only have to cope with our bowling, and appearances can flatter. In any case, we didn't get to see their full panoply as they cruised past us with only two down.

A more ominous aspect of The Royal Oak's cricket was felt and heard almost as soon as they took the field. This was their habit of launching raucous and unanimous appeals for leg before wicket every single time the ball hit the pads — which was often. The phrase 'every single time' is not just a manner of speaking, but literal fact. No matter how far towards square leg the terrified batsman was retreating, the fieldsmen gave every appearance of believing he was smack bang in front of his stumps. Gully and square leg were just as confident as bowler and keeper.

I was standing as umpire at the start of play, and so was subjected to a series of passionate appeals from balls that were clearly going to miss the stumps by several feet. After half a dozen such in the first few overs, bitter resentment began to manifest itself amongst the disgruntled fielders, as the conviction settled in yet again that here was another pack of cheats who weren't going to give anything out. Strident abuse soon followed. After twenty minutes or so I happily handed over my duties to another stern denier of their entreaties. The antics continued for the whole day, and their demeanour in victory showed just how much they relished the satisfaction of outraged injury when they were able to rub our cheating noses in the dirt.

Boorish and antagonistic as The Royal Oak's behaviour certainly was, it was not necessarily an unprofitable tactic in a park cricket competition where more than one umpire seems to act on the assumption that one in three appeals must be out. And their habitual practice certainly paid off handsomely in the Grand Final.

The Royal Oak, in fact, were an extreme example of a common scourge of park cricket—and one that is not unknown at even the highest levels of the game. In NOBs' first two seasons, games against Mill Park were accepted as a necessary punishment to be endured, and other teams here and there played as if the proverbial sheep-stations were at stake. But The Royal Oak were in a class of their own. There are various vernacular phrases to describe such teams, of which 'mongrel bastards' is merely the most complimentary. Whatever competition they had been in the year before was not the first to have kicked them out — and they were not to survive for a second season in the Northern and Combined Churches. Expelled from one competition, they would enrol in another, which would naturally require them to establish their bona fides by working their way up the grades.

The fact that The Royal Oak actually had some pretty handy cricketers meant that they were competing at a level well below their true ability, so to the truculence of their normal behaviour was added total contempt for their puny opponents.

The peculiarlities of the draw spared us a second encounter during the regular season, but we were destined to meet them again in the Grand Final.

Before the season had started it was decided to spare Geoff Crossman the tiresome duty of showing up for Association meetings once a month. By unanimous agreement he had been elevated from Secretary to General Manager in an effort to find a title befitting his girth, and it was accepted that he should be relieved of the main duty of the post, as we all filled in, turn and turn about, to spend a Monday evening bored to tears in order to avoid the club fine for non-attendance.

On the first occasion I reluctantly filled the gap I discovered an unexpected spark of interest during one part of the evening's proceedings. The second time I was delegated I waited for this moment and was not disappointed. This was where the gentleman in charge of the umpiring side of things read out the list of reports lodged and fines exacted since the last meeting. The Royal Oak occupied most of this segment, and added variety and colour to the usual drab array of juvenile petulance, which was the best that other clubs could manage.

At one of the two meetings I attended, The Royal Oak also sent a delegate, and I think their cause was not improved when, after the list of charges had been read out, he wished to make an explanation to the President of the Association, excusing their behaviour on the grounds that the umpire who had reported them was a 'f----arsehole'. This explanation was received very much in the spirit in which it was given.

One startling fact was that The Royal Oak's reserve grade team (it was enough of a shock to find out there was a level even below ours) stank in the nostrils even more than the side we played against. The list of charges was a marvel to behold—not just disputing decisions and abusing the umpires, but tackling the batsmen as they ran between wickets, and the slip fielders amusing themselves by throwing stones at the batsman as the bowler was running in to bowl.

Clearly a Grand Final against such an outfit was going to be eventful. As it turned out, we were lucky to be playing in the grade we were, since at the same time the Royal Oak's reserves were engaged in the D1 Grand Final against a mob we also encountered in our grade calling themselves, but not much resembling, Northern Sportsmen. In D grade, the Royal Oak had knocked the Sportsmen out in the semis, so the D1 Grand Final was to take on the atmosphere of a grudge match.

The President's Report for the season carried a paragraph that could almost have been aimed at us, hinting at dark goings-on:

> I need not remind most of you that cricket and alcohol, during the hours of play, do not mix on or off the field. The association rules have tried to reflect that. However after an incident during a final we have found it necessary to alter the rules to be more stringent.

On turning the page one encoutered among the list of Tribunal Decisions several choice items:

> D. W––, Royal Oak—suspended in his absence for drinking alcohol during hours of play, two matches. Tribunal also recommended club be reprimanded for not attending tribunal.[2]

---

2   How The Royal Oak had got themselves into the Tribunal's good books is a mystery, but this reprimand seems more than generous in view of the fact that some kid in the Under 16s ('bad language and failing to give name to umpire when asked') was suspended indefinitely until he did turn up to face the Tribunal.

J. K–– and E. S––, Northern Sportsmen's Club—suspended for two matches each for drinking alcohol during hours of play.
Royal Oak C.C.—found guilty of frivolous appeals, bad language, unruly behaviour during D1 final.
Royal Oak and Northern Sportsmen's Club—supporters were proved to be drinking alcohol and fighting during final. Tribunal recommends that neither club be readmitted to association until they give an undertaking that no alcohol will be consumed in the vicinity of any game they participate in.[3]

In time we were to fall foul of the new stringency. A season or so later, two of our casual supporters, Dave Horn and Chris the Parkville Postmaster, headed off from Naughton's with a small supply of cans to sit in the sun and watch NOBs at play. The official umpire came over to where they were sitting and ordered them to leave, otherwise we would be kicked out of the competition forthwith. They retreated to the bar, with indignant tales of this high-handed behaviour. Publican Simon Byrne had a simple solution: 'Why didn't you say you were barracking for the other team and get them kicked out?'

But to return to the 1982–83 season. It is something of a mystery how we made the finals at all that year, since we lost more than we won. Two losses to Fairfield Salvation Army, our opponents the season before when the Fairlea breakout occurred, and two more to the Northern Sportsmen would seem to put quite a few teams in front of us. (One reason for feeling the Northerners were not quite so sporting was the experience—the only one in the present writer's career—of fielding out to a double century.)

---

3   NCCCA Annual Report, 1982–83 season.

In between times we must have put in a few reasonable perform-ances, and somewhere in there we had a sequence of three matches where we put up century opening partnerships. It is characteristic of our solid consistency and our determination to stick to the team's game plan that these three partnerships should have been put together by six different opening batsmen.

We also maintained our edge over West Lalor. Even though they had a good enough season to finish second on the ladder, we knocked them over both times we played them, and our victory in the last home and home game lifted us to fourth spot and earned us a crack at them again next week in the semi-final.

West Lalor was one team we happily drank with after the day's play, and over a few beers they put us straight about where we stood. Never mind previous results—they were second and we were fourth. A 'no result' game—such as one team batting from start to finish with no reply possible, or more probably the whole match being rained out—would mean they went into the Grand Final. They batted well down the list, and they let us know that when they won the toss they would bat for the full two days.

Unfortunately for their plans, the spin of the coin went the other way and captain Steve Loney decided we would have first hit. Horsburgh made a hundred, Mick Butera contributed a nice 42, and at stumps on the first day we were well placed at 9 down for a little more than 250. Since we had to get West Lalor all out in one after-noon to win, it was automatic that we would close at the overnight score in order to give ourselves as much time as possible—or so West Lalor thought.

Before the start of play on the second Saturday, even as their own openers were strapping on the pads, they saw our two not out bats-men padding up again, and they were incredulous to the point of incoherence. In utter stupefaction they tried to point out to us the extent of our folly—didn't we understand the rules?

As things turned out, the end of our innings didn't take long coming, Pat O'Connor running true to form at Number 11. It wasn't the number of extra runs so much as the total unexpectedness of it that flabbergasted West Lalor. They started their innings in a fog of bewilderment and never recovered equilibrium. In under an hour we'd rolled them for 32—Rob Dyhin 6 for 12 and Steve Loney 3 for 16.

Two unexpected factors assisted us in our comprehensive victory, one an act of (more-or-less) God, the other to be laid entirely at West Lalor's door. Early in the intervening week a water main had burst in St George's Road near our Alma Mater, Northcote High School, flooding Merri Park where the game was taking place. So whereas we batted on a dustbowl where every tap could fly to the boundary, the abundant grass of the second week slowed scoring considerably, and the lush atmosphere helped the ball swing all over the place.

This would not have made such a decisive difference between the sides had not West Lalor, in a show of confidence not just bordering on but exceeding foolhardiness, organised a club night at the trots on the Friday evening. All members had dutifully turned out, and more than a couple had kicked on to an all-night poker game. So when they were compelled, against expectations, to take the field at start of play, they did so as a bedraggled and depleted unit, several of the team having decided that the opening batsmen would be occupying the crease and they needn't be excessively punctual.

One of the latecomers—and one of their best batsmen—was known to all his teammates as Motor Boat. As mentioned earlier, West Lalor had a full array of nicknames, and some time previously we had learned that this particular soubriquet derived from his spluttering mode of speech when totally intoxicated—'but-but-but-but-but'. On this occasion we were able to verify its accuracy. Radio commentators who say a batsman 'failed to trouble the scorers' do not take account of the flurry of entries required to register a first ball dismissal, such as Motor Boat's on this occasion.

It was still well before the scheduled tea break, but West Lalor rightly felt that the task of knocking off the 230 odd deficit, establishing a lead, and getting us all out before 6 o'clock was a bit far fetched, so the two teams headed for the pub—with several West Lalor players still asking why we'd batted on.

It wasn't just the margin that was surprising. Few of us had counted on victory at all, and we faced the prospect of a Grand Final without the core of our team. In particular, our two star recruits for the season had made other arrangements. Rob Dyhin, who'had topped the bowling averages and was second in the batting, couldn't make it for either weekend of the game, and Peter Horsburgh, top of the batting and second in the bowling, certainly couldn't play the first day of the game. This made a fair hole in our team, and The Royal Oak had more reasons than they knew to be confident of the outcome.

The Grand Final traditionally takes in the Labor Day holiday, so there are two Saturdays of play from a quarter to two to six o'clock, and the intervening Monday, 10.30 to 6—longer even than a Test match day. Horsburgh could play on the Monday and the second Saturday, but we would be short on the first day. I was to field sub for him, but his absence meant we were without a spinner of any kind for The Royal Oak's first innings.

In fact, of the side that took the field only Steve and Biddo qualified as bowlers at all. Biddo had had an excellent season with the ball, taking well over 20 wickets, but this was not to be his day. Earlier in his career, Biddo's consistency had been interrupted by those occasions when he would spend the afternoon inviting his teammates to contemplate with him the wonderful shade of green in the grass.[5] On such days it was best to dispatch him to a remote part of the outfield and hope the ball didn't get hit there too often. It's unlikely he'd been on the same stuff this time, but he bowled like it. Steve, however, had a day out.

Once again, it was up to us to get The Royal Oak out, and, batting first, they could afford to continue for as long as they liked. Word was going around—whether accurate or not—that one of their opening batsman was averaging something over 200 for the season. This must have meant he'd been not out quite a few times, but he'd also scored a poultice of runs.

Steve took the new ball, and the first delivery of the Grand Final pitched on a length, evaded the defensive bat and just lifted the off bail. The batsman's reaction was more or less what you'd expect, though few disappointed hopefuls can have managed to get their bat over the boundary line from quite so close to the centre of the ground.

In no time Steve—entirely unaided—had knocked the top off The Oak's batting and they were 5 for about 20. They did bat all the way down, however, and probably none of them had given us the edge Motor Boat and his mates had done a week earlier. Numbers six and seven proceeded to make a bit of a stand—not without unmerited good fortune. Early on in the partnership, I was fielding at point only about ten yards from the bat when the batsman hit the ball straight to me and called for a run. I thought, 'They won't even cross,' as I bent to pick up the ball.

Mention has been made elsewhere of the condition of the grounds on which we played. Without a drop of rain for months, Donath Reserve was a maze of parched cracks, some several inches wide. About two feet from my hand, the ball running briskly along the

---

4   Biddo entirely denies the truth of this scurrilous story and claims that monumental hangovers left him feeling that reclining on the greensward was far preferable to chasing a cricket ball. Pat O'Connor, however, having decided on character assassination, persists in his version of events.

ground struck a crack and took off, whizzing past my right ear. There was absolutely no chance of stopping it, so I felt somewhat aggrieved that the official umpire should make so free as to volunteer the comment to everyone within earshot, 'That was a bad mistake.'

The umpire's role is to be the object of abuse, not dish it out. And their performance for the match will come in for comment in the next few pages.

Having got themselves back in the game, The Royal Oak proceeded to build a total, and things were set up for the team slogger coming in at Number 10. He laid about him to such effect that his fifty came up in about half an hour. He showed a willingness to aim the ball high to long on, and after one such blow, Ian Ewing (bowling off breaks, to show just how desperately thin our resources were) asked for a fieldsman on the boundary.

Pat O'Connor was closest, and duly dispatched. That Pat should have been playing in a Grand Final at all was clear proof that form and ability did not influence the selection panel. Or perhaps there was just no one else available. But as Club Founder he had a right to a game whenever he chose. The long weekend usually meant for Pat a trip down to his in-laws at Torquay. Pat was wont to refer to this family hospitality as The Compound, and it seems likely that there was closer supervision of his drinking than was necessarily appreciated.

The Grand Final forced a revision of these plans—too late for Pip to change her arrangements, so Pat would remain in town on his own. Being off the leash on a Friday night for the first time in a long while wrought the expected result. Pat took the field next day wearing sun glasses. Of recent years it has become *de rigeur* for cricketers at the highest level to flaunt fashionable shades, but back in the early eighties they were not sporting accessories. Dark glasses on the field meant one thing only—an almighty hangover.

Pat's fielding for the day had been as shaky as one might have expected, so he was probably not the one to send on a vital errand. The very next ball was lifted in Pat's direction. Pat did not move forward or back, or take a step to either side. The sunglasses meant no one could see his eyes, so we didn't know where he was looking, and some were worried for his safety as the ball flew low and fast. But there was no panic, no cause for alarm, and no trouble at all about taking the catch. A less scrupulous competitor would have hurled the ball skyward and charged towards the wicket in celebration. Perhaps Pat's hangover put a damper on such a display of enthusiasm. Instead, he looked calmly to right and left to establish the position of the boundary flags, and signalled 6. As always, Pat's best work for the club was performed off the field of play.

With a lot of life in the tail, The Royal Oak got away to a very healthy 240, always likely to be a challenge, especially when a couple of quick wickets saw us precariously placed at stumps with three down.

The real killer wicket here, which brought no credit to anyone, was that of Steve Loney—certainly our best batsman, at least until Horsburgh could get there on the Monday.

All day a howling wind had been blowing, and for most of The Royal Oak's innings we had agreed to dispense with the bails, since they kept on being blown off. When our turn came, however, The Royal Oak, in the only sign they ever showed of respecting the punctilio of the game, insisted that the bails be on—even if (or probably because) it meant frequently interrupting the game and the batsman's concentration to pick them up and replace them.

They had a particularly quick young bowler, rated by all of us as just a shade below The Beast of some years before, who was doing severe damage to our batting. He bowled one to Steve that cut back and took him on the right hip, well above stump high and very definitely on the way up, so leg before wicket was out of the question. The ball bounced harmlessly away towards third slip. This did not prevent uproarious appeals from the entire fielding side. Bowler's umpire looked at square leg, both shrugged their shoulders, then bowler's end raised his finger to signify out.

Steve was not one to argue the toss, and I never saw him do so on any other occasion, but he did exclaim in his astonishment, 'How am I out?' The two umpires caucused briefly and said, 'You're out. The bails are on the ground.'

'They've been on the ground all day. That's why we haven't been using them,' said Steve.

'Well, you're still out.' All the while of course the assembled forces of the fielding side (who knew perfectly well what had happened) are screaming in his ear, 'Get off the field, you bloody cheat.'

Steve persisted. 'So what do I tell them to put in the scorebook where it says 'How out'?'

The umpire then made an extraordinary statement: 'Well, we don't really know, but the bails are down so you must have either been bowled or hit your wicket.'

That The Royal Oak, with a historical record and a current performance like theirs, should be the ones to reap the benefit of umpiring uncertainty—against all the Laws of the game—shows how subtly pressure can be applied on officials anxious to demonstrate their total impartiality. Either that or outright intimidation. Take your pick.

Steve withdrew defeated, leaving behind him a set of opponents even more belligerent in their conviction that no one ever played fair and the world had it in for them.

On the Monday everyone got a few, no one enough. Only Ewing and Radcliffe passed 20. One or two more roughies from the umps didn't help either. It's always satisfying to have someone to blame, but just over a hundred short was probably a fair measure of the two teams.

However, it was still not quite lunch, and four of the scheduled seven sessions of the match remained for us to turn things around.

This is where a dedicated team would have dug deep and showed their mettle.

NOBs' reaction, on the other hand, was to send someone over to the huddle where batsmen—one at least intent on heavy revenge—were padding up to say, 'Thanks for the game, chaps. See you next season.'

This was received with some perplexity by the opposition. 'But this is a Grand Final. You can't just throw it in.' Our representative pointed out that the game had already taken place and they'd won. Congratulations.

As we tumbled into various cars for a lightning getaway, we left behind us a bewildered group standing hands on hips, some still wearing a pad or two, staring after us trying to understand what had taken place.

It was clear to us that The Royal Oak were intent on batting through the remaining eight hours and more of play, and that we had nothing much to stop them doing so. Hours later, around the scheduled time for stumps, but after a full afternoon in the pub, one of our team was heading home, his route taking him past Donath Reserve. On reaching home, he gleefully rang those of us left in the pub to report that a couple of forlorn figures were still there at the ground, wanly conducting a net, presumably getting themselves in tune for next season, though in another competition unfortunate enough to embrace them.

An extra source of pleasure to us came when we somehow learned that The Royal Oak had organised a barrel for the next Saturday afternoon to celebrate the victory they were certain of achieving, and we had just pulled the rug from under them.

Sometimes even running away can feel like a victory.

7

With Respect to Umpires

We had always expected to cop a fair hiding in the Grand Final, but had thought it would come from The Royal Oak's fast bowlers and bludgeoning batsmen—two aspects of the game in which we were not entirely disgraced. Where we were comprehensively beaten was in the umpiring. Some of the more self-righteous among us (and I defer to no one in this aspect of the game) nursed a sense of grievance about the treatment we received.

As a team and as individuals, The Royal Oak did nothing to conceal their attitude of surly belligerence and their contempt for all the niceties of the game. After a season full of umpires' reports and suspensions, come the Grand Final, they still got a dream run from the white-coated officials. It made us wonder what you have to do to get yourself a bad reputation.

And yet a moment's reflection might have suggested that the distinctive psychology of umpires supplies the explanation. The task is so thankless that anyone prepared to undertake it must be imbued with a sense of noble service to the great game, someone who has swallowed all the propaganda so carefully nurtured over such a long time about the ennobling qualities of the most gentlemanly of sports and the bracing moral uplift to be derived from strenuous competition. A team like NOBs, intent on enjoying its Saturday in the sun, is never going to win the approval of the sort of person temperamentally inclined towards umpiring. Our attitude was an implicit rebuke to the sacrifice he felt he had made. No team could have more clearly demonstrated than NOBs did that we had entirely abandoned the competitive ethic, being indeed quite happy to walk away if the game didn't seem worth the candle.

The Royal Oak, by way of contrast, scrapped like sewer rats, and no one could miss the fact that they were competitive. No higher ideal existed for them. Obviously their approach to the game constituted a better method of getting your own way with umpires than ours.

Perhaps a subtle reverse psychology also underlay their boorish intimidation. In any other social context, the instinctive and entirely reasonable reaction to such aggression would be self-defence, allied to the thought, 'I'm not going to give in to these mongrels.' But umpires are obsessed with delusions about fair play. It was as if they gritted their teeth and resolved to show their detractors that they were unmoved by insults and would dispense justice without fear or favour. They thus leant over backwards to be even-handed, and leaning over backwards is not the ideal method for seeing quite what is going on in front of you. And anyway, their efforts to be strictly impartial gained no gratitude at all from The Royal Oak, whose trucu-lent resentment was undiminished. However muddled their perform-ance on this occasion, the umpires were as always a reminder of the noble ideal of fair play, which is enshrined in the mythology of cricket—an ideal regularly brought to grief on cricket grounds stretch-ing all the way from Lord's to Donath Reserve, Thomastown.

And yet it is true that cricket, even in its darkest hours, keeps alive the flame of its fond illusions. Rightly so, for cricket is at the pinna-cle of team games, the embodiment in phrase and fable of all that is noble in human endeavour.

Though this mythology bears little relationship to the way the game is actually played at any level, it is nevertheless powerful enough to have served as a populist prop for a succession of Prime Ministers. Imperial nostalgia on the one hand and colonial cockiness on the other have made the game equally useful to Right and Left.

Only one of these self-proclaimed devotees had actually played the game even at a standard rivalling NOBs, and all anyone knows about his prowess is that he broke his glasses and nearly blinded himself trying to prove he was still one of the boys.

Those responsible for the public face of cricket assiduously pro-mote its sanctified image in the face of unruly reality, and tend to back it up with a generalised notion about a supposed English genius for games. The fact that tennis, soccer, badminton, Rugby of various kinds, billiards and you name it are played by rules (only cricket has Laws!) originally devised in England does not necessarily indicate a peculiar national talent for devising forms of competitive sport. Every human community has had its semi-organised pastimes that involve throwing, hitting, kicking balls of various shapes and sizes and de-grees of hardness. With soccer in mind, one could observe that only the English would have developed a game that makes a key strategy out of hitting the ball with your head. Sensible people make a point of avoiding that particular hazard.

In fact, the distinctive English contribution was the devising of fastidious sets of rules to inhibit the free flowing spontaneity of such activities and then insisting that everyone else had to stick to what they had written down, any infringement of which was clearly 'cheating'. The English genius was not for sport but for bureaucracy.

In consequence the English have a traditional hostility to continental flamboyance. Eric Cantona may have single-handedly rescued English soccer from *rigor mortis*, but there was never any doubt he was fundamentally unacceptable. He was so far outside the pale that he was even known to argue with umpires, respect for umpires being the supreme virtue in English publicity, if not in practice.[1] As anyone acquainted with the history of cricket knows, the two great constants down the years have been ceaseless antagonism between players and administrators, and feuds over who should be allowed to umpire and how well or poorly they did their job.

Cricket can, however, lay claim to being the most English of games by virtue of a set of Laws of mind-numbing complexity. To look at sample questions a prospective umpire must be able to answer to qualify for his ticket is to marvel at circumstances of almost inconceivable improbability that someone has carefully foreseen and written a regulation to cover. Aficionados have never ceased to regret the decision of the Marylebone Cricket Club about twenty years ago to remove the antique elegance of phrasing in an attempt to make the Laws comprehensible to persons who understand the English language. If the process continues even Test players may get to know the rules—though that day seems a long way off.

At the end of his career, Australia's longest serving wicketkeeper, Rod Marsh, showed himself unaware of the rules concerning a pretty basic aspect of his craft—how to run a batsman out when the wicket

---

1   Cantona also earned a degree of celebrity by hurdling the boundary fence in an effort to kick a spectator in the head. From all one knows about English soccer crowds, this seems not only reasonable but restrained.

has already been broken. Both batsmen found themselves at the bowler's end, and Marsh had the ball in his glove—but the bails were already on the ground. He yanked a stump from the ground with his left hand and bashed it against the ball in his right glove.

A batsman conversant with the rules could have strolled the twenty-two yards and casually completed the run, but on this occasion the batsman was as befuddled as Marsh and meekly walked off the ground. The umpire was not called on for a decision and did not feel moved to intervene, though the Laws are perfectly clear that this was not a legitimate form of dismissal.

A more hilarious episode occurred in the West Indies in 1995, where Dean Jones contrived to get himself run out walking off the ground, having been bowled by what he didn't realise was a no-ball. There were not one but two Laws of the game clearly specifying he was not out in the circumstances, but amnesia descended upon the umpires, and after only 200 odd Tests between them you could hardly expect Jones himself or Border at the other end to know the rules.[2] It was rumoured that some of the West Indians did, but kept quiet about it. Such happy incidents all combine to enhance the noble reputation of the greatest and most gentlemanly of games.

What makes an umpire? It must be the case that ageing players unable to let go of the passion of their youth form the bulk of the fraternity—certainly at the humble levels where we competed. In

---

2   Law 38.2, which states that a batsman can be run out off a no-ball only if actually attempting a run, was a very recent addition, the direct result of an unpleasant incident in a match in which Border himself played: a Test vs Pakistan in Melbourne in 1978–79. Rodney Hogg was run out by Javed Miandad off a no-ball while absent-mindedly patting the pitch. The episode (including Hogg's riposte of knocking over his stumps) was widely discussed, as was the subsequent change in the Laws, so Border's ignorance is doubly surprising.

England, the panel of first class umpires contains many former players taking a lingering farewell from the game, but in Australia this is very rare. Our leading umpires seem to have recognised at quite an early age that they weren't going to make it as a player and chosen an alternative way of getting themselves noticed. From the far side of the fence, there does seem to be a more genial air of tolerance in the way an English umpire administers the game. An air of fractious self-importance is a common character defect of those who are uncomfortably aware that they have tumbled into authority over their natural superiors.

Low self-esteem can do terrible things to people, and it was clearly a serious error by those who framed the Laws of Cricket that they should have relegated umpires to Law Number 3. Players come first, and even substitute fieldsmen and those who run between wickets for injured batsmen are given precedence over the august duties of the umpire. But certainly the Laws of cricket require two umpires to officiate in every game.[3]

When one considers the abundance of games of cricket that take place every weekend for six months of the year, it is apparent that the supply of people with sufficient interest and stamina to spend four hours every Saturday afternoon standing up in the summer sun, or perhaps on the blasted heath when the early spring winds blow in off the ice cap, is quickly exhausted.

Mingled with the above delights is the reward of being shouted at, first imploringly and then abusively, by two sets of strapping young chaps who all feel you're a useless old fart, obviously incapable of any kind of physical performance yourself, and probably half-blind.

---

3   Umpires—not referees. Referees adjudicate disputes: umpires by linguistic derivation are without peer and therefore beyond question. The recent invention of a match referee in addition to the umpires for first class games is an admission of defeat, and follows hard upon the end of civilisation as we know it—which, as every cricket follower is aware, occurred on Saturday 30 August 1980 during the Centenary Test at Lord's when a member of the MCC laid violent hands upon Umpire David Constant, not only within the Members' Reserve but at the very portals of the Long Room.

The game's loftiest administrators are keenly aware of the treatment dished out to these honest servants by the rude mechanicals who do the actual playing, and regularly implore the latter to behave a little better. A typical example survives in the club records: a circular sent out in October 1989 by the Victorian Cricket Association to all clubs in all official competitions, stating *inter alia*, 'You would be well aware of the acute shortage of umpires for cricket. One of the problems of course in not only recruiting umpires, but retaining them, is that of abuse that they sometimes receive from players at all levels, be they senior or junior teams.' Since the whole competition was destined to fold at the end of the season, we were given little time to alter our sorry ways and make amends to the offended parties.

But then again, why should players apologise for the mistakes of those long dead who created the game, and the still-living (some of them) administrators who are responsible for its ongoing maintenance? What is now Law 27 states very clearly that 'The umpires shall not give a batsman out unless appealed to.' No one has ever suggested that polite diffidence is the best way of convincing an umpire that the ball has just brushed the edge of a defensive bat, or that the pad is slap bang in front of middle peg. Cricket is thus the only game that not only permits but positively *requires* the players to shout at the umpire. And once debate has been initiated, who is to say where the cut and thrust of Socratic dialogue may lead?

Though NOBs may not have led the charge, it strains belief to imagine we were entirely blameless in the matter of dishing out gratuitous insults to umpires. But I do believe we were not so crass as to take advantage of the obvious vulnerability of one umpire we encountered occasionally, a well-known figure in the Northern and Combined Churches—unmistakable, really, given that he had a glass eye (which could become disconcertingly skewed in the exertions of a long afternoon) and a walking stick. He must have known better than anyone how spiteful park cricket can be, so it was a sign of genuine courage that he should present himself week after week and season after season to be the target of small-minded abuse. Then again, originality and wit are in short supply on the field, so he'd heard them all before and probably had a better riposte than any insult a peevish bowler could come up with.

Blindness and physical debility are traditional insults. When the chat turns to sexual preferences you know things are becoming poisonous. Tolerance of minority tastes is not automatically to be expected among park cricketers, for this is a loudly heterosexual culture. There was one umpire in particular who was the subject of dark mutterings. The story came back from one of our opponents, whose business took him on a regular round of the second-hand shops of Melbourne's north, that he had dropped into a furniture disposal warehouse in Preston and was surprised to see the familiar umpire arm in arm with a loudly dressed and brightly painted transvestite. Recognition was mutual, but the umpire's reaction was to bolt headlong out of the shop, leaving his (so to speak) lady friend to assess the possibilities for redecorating the lounge room. Thereafter the unfortunate umpire's moral authority was somewhat diminished whenever he was required to officiate in West Lalor games—a team we found always favoured plain speaking and the direct statement.

Given the hazards of the job, it is a wonder that anyone undertakes it at all. Of course a regular few bob in the hip pocket about which the Taxation Department need not be told is an inducement to some, but it is not surprising that, after the needs of District cricket in all its grades, sub-district spreading below that, and various other competitions of some degree of seriousness have been met, by the time you arrive at D Grade Churches it is remarkable that anyone is willing to watch and pass judgement upon the earnest incompetence with which we go about our business. Generally in park cricket we have to conduct the game in the absence of neutral officials, leaving the duties to be performed by the players themselves. The inevitable clash of expectations can lend an edge of raw excitement to a pleasant Saturday afternoon, and will be discussed later in this chapter. But even at the lowest level from time to time you arrive at a game to find a real live official umpire, with a cloth badge fastened with a safety pin, or (if he is married to an understanding wife) tacked with a hasty running stitch, to his white coat.

Indeed, NOBs may have been more generously served in the provision of umpires on account of our anomalous status as a pub team in a Church competition. Certainly the umpires' advisor was one dignitary with whom we came to have a more than nodding acquaintance. With some regularity, he would turn up at our match, ostensibly on a chance visit to cast a supervising eye over how the umpires were handling proceedings.

But from our point of view—and we were not mistaken in this—the umpires' advisor arrived not to look at the umpires but to look at us. Though we prided ourselves on playing with exemplary fairness, those in authority were slow to recognise it, and a pub team was inevitably viewed with suspicion by the pew warmers, so we were kept on a tight rein. For the brief period in which The Royal Oak flourished in our competition we were granted the luxury of an umpire far more frequently than random chance would have allowed. Whatever reputation we might have established over five or six years in the competition did not survive one season of The Royal Oak's behaviour, and as the only other pub team at that time we were immediately tarred with their brush. Considering the sparse resources available to the Association as a whole, and how many games of far greater moment were in progress, it must have been galling to the administrators to have to delegate a high proportion of the available umpires to keeping a couple of D Grade pub teams in order, but for a season or so NOBs had to tolerate the vagaries of our opponents' decisions less often than we otherwise would.

Not that it was necessarily an unmixed blessing to have a qualified umpire. At least when the opposing team does the job you know where you stand, but a significant number of park cricket umpires seem to have hit on the same formula for keeping both sides happy— namely, every third appeal is out. So the hairsbreath decision is judiciously turned down, but two overs later an irresponsible shout sees the batsman rifled out with no recourse. The inconsistency can be off-putting for both teams. Not to speak of the undeserved benefits heaped on teams who appeal for everything.

Furthermore, some official umpires seem drawn to the task by an authoritarian cast of mind, determined to break fractious players on the anvil of their own indomitable will. One such I recall in the South Suburban comp. It was a miserable, cold afternoon, spitting rain throughout, punctuated by occasional deluges. Never once did this stern master feel we had earned the right to withdraw from the field as he kept us bound to our duty, despite the combined pleas of batsmen, bowlers and fielders. It was like being back at school.

And when the darkness of the night settled in early, and every other game taking place across the broad expanse of Albert Park had sensibly rolled their mats and gone home, our King Lear among umpires would not countenance any suggestion that the light wasn't quite up to scratch, and I think actually reported a couple of players from each side who made their views known.

Close to scheduled stumps I was fulfilling the supernumerary duty at square leg when, as an ironic protest against the utter unreasonableness of what was going on, someone in our team switched his car lights on. This was a very modest advance towards the Holy Grail— day/night cricket—but I suppose I can claim to have been there when the seed was sown. I had my back turned at the moment the switch was thrown, but the sudden illumination made a significant difference to general visibility. I'm not sure the umpire didn't threaten to report whoever it was spoiling his fun for the evening.

It crossed my mind that one way I could hasten things to a sensible close would be to call 'no ball' from square leg as every delivery was bowled, pleading as excuse that the Laws of the game required me to be 'entirely satisfied of the absolute fairness of a delivery' and that since I couldn't see the bowler I couldn't be sure. But this seemed likely to cause more aggravation than it was worth—especially as I was not one of the batsmen likely to get his head knocked off.

As far as I could see, in that competition, common sense was not one of the qualities assessed in awarding the umpire's badge. It may even have been the same season as the previous incident when we were playing in a Semi-final—so the outcome was significant to us, though ranking very low in the overall affairs of human kind. But a sense of proportion is the last thing one can count on in park cricket.

We were chasing a very makeable target a bit over 200 when a wicket fell which brought the best batsman we had in the team in to bat. Though a very experienced cricketer, he contrived a way of getting out without facing a ball that no one present had ever encountered before.

Standing at the bowler's end, he answered his partner's call for a single and made his ground comfortably before the throw came in from the deep field. The keeper wasn't quite good enough to glove the throw cleanly, and the ball bounced around a bit before coming to rest in the blockhole just as the newly arrived batsman stepped up to take middle and leg in order to commence his innings. It seemed both courteous and mutually convenient to pick the ball up and hand it to the wicket keeper, still running in circles trying to recover from his inept handling. The keeper, however, had a different view and loudly appealed to the umpire for a 'Handled the Ball' dismissal. Quick as a flash, the alert official fired the batsman out.

It was all so sudden that those of us watching from the boundary didn't have a clue what had happened. As the defeated hero shuffled off the ground someone suggested, 'Perhaps he forgot his box'— 'Does he need another set of gloves?'

'I'm out,' he said, as soon as he got close enough for anyone to hear, though each time he said it there seemed to be more colourful and varied words in between the *I'm* and the *out*.

It is true that at the time these events occurred the Laws of Cricket gave umpires no discretion in such matters, and there was no provision for a captain to withdraw an appeal once made, even if he wanted to. A decision had to be made strictly by the book—and it seems difficult to stretch interpretations far enough to find a justification in the Laws for calling the ball 'dead' in the circumstances that had occurred.

However, decisions in park cricket are seldom referred to the International Commission for Human Justice, and surely an umpire with half a brain might just have skated over the strict provisions of the Law and asked the captain whether or not it was an appeal that had been made or did his team intend to conduct the rest of the game like a pack of mongrels?

Certainly, when something similar happened in a Test Match a couple of years later,[4] the Laws were swiftly changed so that now the fielding captain is allowed to intervene to withdraw an overly hasty or overly vindictive appeal made by one of his underlings.

Signing the score book at stumps, the opposing captain did feel moved to mumble an apology. The fact that he had done and said

---

4   Andrew Hilditch, in Perth in 1979, handed a wayward lobbed return to the bowler, Sarfraz Nawaz, who then appealed, repeatedly and passionately, to the umpire. This match followed hard on the heels of Hogg–Miandad incident (see footnote, page 118). Hilditch was opening the batting immediately after Alan Hirst had ended the Pakistani innings by doing a Mankad on their number 11, Sikhander Bakht. Had Hilditch played a bit more park cricket, he would have known not to give an aggravated opposition even the smell of a chance of cheating you out. In D Grade we knew, if the opposition was on the warpath, no acts of casual politeness were permitted.

nothing at the time, and that the incident had played its part in helping his team sneak into the Grand Final was taken into account in our
assessment of his sincerity. The umpire in question packed his kit
and left without a word. One fact that struck me at the time was how
remarkably young he looked—too young surely to have played much
cricket himself, or to have any idea of the general spirit in which the
game should be conducted.

For the most part, however, umpires present a more autumnal aspect, being drawn from the ranks of ex-players seeking to prolong
their youthful diversions.

One of the saddest examples of this I remember from my days in
the Sydney Churches' Competition. There was one team we played
regularly in our local sector of C Grade, St Aidan's, Annandale, I
think they were. They were mostly grizzled veterans—or so they
seemed to me at age 16, a wide-eyed boy from the bush.

They had clearly found a level of cricket at which they were entirely comfortable—playing against mostly young kids of very me-
diocre ability. They thrashed us every time, and usually won our section of C Grade. After doing so they would put in a plea to the Association—along the lines that six of their best players were retiring or
moving interstate—and ask not to be promoted to B Grade.

Next season they would all front up again and knock the stuffing
out of us as usual.

When I played my first game for Petersham Bappos our attack
was opened by two 14-year-olds, and the Christian gentlemen of St
Aidan's showed no mercy whatsoever.

By my last season we still had the same opening bowlers, but at
18 they bowled like the wind. (One of them was that year selected as
pitcher in the New South Wales baseball squad for the Claxton Shield,
so he had a natural turn of speed with the ball in hand.)

Timbrell Park, where we played most of our games, lies on the
shores of Iron Cove, and whatever the weather elsewhere, there is

always a hefty breeze either onshore or off. Our turn to play St Aidan's came around. We batted first and concluded our innings late on the first Saturday, just time for a couple of overs at them before stumps. One of the opening batsmen, accustomed to easy pickings off us, was disconcerted to find the ball going past without him getting a sight of it. This happened a couple of times in the first over before one lively bouncer struck him on the temple, and he was assisted from the field with blood flowing profusely.

Being a hardy chap, he fronted next week and came in at the fall of the next wicket—which was not long in occurring. The wind had switched round from the preceding Saturday, and he found himself facing the other opening bowler, now also coming downwind. First ball took him full pitch on the left foot before he had moved from his stance. This time he was carried off with broken bones and did not venture a third appearance.

Some weeks later we were preparing for our game, when we were accosted by the umpire allocated to us—none other than the now ex-opening bat from St Aidan's. If the pleasure he derived from his Saturday afternoons was somewhat diminished of late, we were certain that we had assisted him in making a wise career choice.

One ex-NOB at least did don the white coat in his retirement. Graham Baird played a mere half game for us, but since that one Saturday was the day of the Fairlea breakout he has his place on the club's honour roll. His enlistment in the ranks of the enemy came at a time subsequent to his brief but eventful career with us, and to his sudden translation from Auckland clean across the civilised world to the goldfields of Western Australia.

Of a Saturday, Kalgoorlie offers diversions so rich and varied that standing up in the desert sun all day seemed to Graham one of the more attractive options. He duly passed the exam and the eye test (there is one, but as every cricketer knows it fails entirely in its purpose) and qualified himself to stand in matches conducted under the auspices of the Eastern Goldfields Cricket Association.[5] He thus unwittingly embroiled himself in an industrial struggle that, in terms of the principles at stake and the outraged honour of the injured party, must rank high even in the turbulent history of Kalgoorlie.

The mining industry operates on shift work, so no team can be sure it will have the same set of players two Saturdays running. As a result, all matches are one day games. Down the pit they're used to a hard day's work, so EGCA games were no afternoon picnic, but an all-day marathon, 60 overs a side, belting along at about 18 overs an hour, starting at 10 o'clock and running until 6 if necessary. Normal conditions included temperatures in the high 30s. A lunch break was scheduled from 12.30 to 1.20.

It was the luncheon adjournment that brought about the confrontation of mighty adversaries, though this time it was the silvertails and not the rank and file who pulled the plug.

The players, being the footsloggers of the game, usually made do with a bundle from the local fish and chip shop, or sandwiches prepared by a supportive wife. The umpires, however, men of dignity and standing in the community, would characteristically repair to the bosom of their family for a sit-down meal carefully timed to fit the break between innings. A contributing factor may have been that it was safer to establish a certain distance from aggrieved players.

Around 1991, a new President with a new broom took over the Association, and some way into the season forced through a pet reform of his own, which was to shorten the lunch break from 50 to 20 minutes. This may have been intended to abbreviate a long day for everyone involved, but the umpires, who after all are the only ones who have to be out in the sun for every gruelling minute, bitterly resented two things—not being consulted; and being demoted from roast lamb to hamburgers.

---

5   As always for Sandgropers, the word 'Eastern' was a purely relative term meaning 'not quite as far west as everything else'.

At a meeting of the Umpires' Association the President of the Cricket Association was unanimously voted to be a 'goose' (a term, I am informed, of more potent significance in the Kalgoorlie argot than in Standard Australian usage) and the Umpires' President was delegated to have matters out with him at a meeting arranged for the Federal Hotel.

The 'Feddie' is Kalgoorlie's roughest pub, where the scantily clad barmaids can, on the flip of a coin, be induced to add new distractions to the post-match beer. The conversation between the twin supremos of cricket on the Eastern Goldfields is reliably reported not to have diminished the hotel's reputation in any way, and the result was a suspension of relations between the two bodies—umpires refusing to stand, players refusing to notice the difference.

A union man to his bootstraps (as well as to his black trousers, white coat, tie, panama hat and official badge), Graham joined the strikers. It was scarcely an option for the small but solid band of umpires to form a picket line around the picket fence of every cricket ground in Kalgoorlie, but Graham did his bit on the first Saturday of the dispute by cycling past a neighbouring ground on his way to an early start in the pub (not the Feddie, of course) and paused briefly to observe the blackleg operations.

Not only was a match taking place, but there were clearly to be seen white clad players leaning on bats at square leg and white clad gentlemen behind the bowler's wicket carefully turning down all appeals for leg before wicket.

The demarcation dispute continued for the rest of the season, with the umpires maintaining that no runs were scored or wickets taken during that period. Perhaps the Association still keeps two sets of career figures for those who played through the eventful season— runs scored with umpires, and inflated figures for the period when you could rely on your mates for a bit of help.

At the end of the season, the reforming President was relieved of his responsibilities and a somewhat chastened Association made its peace with the umpires. Graham, however, was not one of those who assisted in the resurgence of the game on the Goldfields. Having learned what he should always have known as a player—how little umpires' services are valued by those who use them—he took his bat and ball home and confined his subsequent cricketing activities to the backyard.

It is unfortunately true that cricket teams are off-hand, even contemptuous, towards those who sacrifice their leisure to play their part in enabling the minor drama of park cricket to proceed. Umpires are at best a necessary encumbrance, at worst the rightful targets of abuse and hatred, and the arrogance of youth finds it difficult to conceive that these lonely souls are human beings like the rest of us, prey to the hopes and fears of our common human lot: 'If you prick us, do we not bleed?'

Once at least NOBs were forcefully reminded that umpires are not to be taken entirely for granted. Play was not so riveting as to keep everyone's attention caught up in the unfolding action and, as is characteristic, the close to the wicket fieldsmen were engaged in desultory conversation in no way related to the game in progress. Wicketkeeper Radcliffe asked his attendant slippers what they'd had for dinner the night before. It must have been an exotic night out for several of them, as satay prawns turned out to have been a popular choice. As one topic led to another and natural depravity took over, the idle enquiry was made, 'Did anyone get a root last night?'

First slip, second and gully all replied in the negative. What about the batsman? Again, no. Feeling that the enquiry should be broadened, Max asked the bowler to pause in his run-up and, without coarsely shouting to fieldsmen on the boundary at third man and fine leg, posed the question more generally, 'Did anyone here get a root last night?'

Modestly but definitely the umpire raised his hand, the only one amongst us to claim the distinction. He had seemed a decrepit old man to us previously, but play proceeded with new respect for our accomplished official.

It was rare that an umpire should impose a distinctive identity on the game, one being much like another. But certainly no one else was quite like the chirpy little chappie who, during the tea interval, would produce a ukulele from his kit bag and regale us all with George Formby numbers until play resumed. This was not his only oddity, as he always carried with him a bowling marker, which he would entrust to the opening bowler saying, 'Don't lose that, son. It's been used by Ian Meckiff.' And he would append two or three other names whose past distinction added lustre to his aluminium disc.

We succeeded in not losing it on him, so if he's still raising the finger and strumming his instrument he is still presumably handing out the marker, saying, 'Don't lose that, son. It's been used by Ian Meckiff and Clem Simonetto.'

Banjo playing on the boundary was an aberration, however, because these are serious men, fully aware of the gravity of their responsibilities. I well remember the deep pondering of one of their number when I approached him for the formality of his signature on the scorebook. It was the end of the first final we ever played in, at Mayer Park in Thornbury, against East Thomastown. Steady rain on the second day removed any faint chance of victory we might have had. More realistically, it spared most of the team the terrifying prospect of facing The Beast coming downhill, all restraint thrown to the wind in this sudden death confrontation.

It was a game we were never going to win, so there were no deep regrets as I scribbled out the final scores with the note, 'Game washed out.' I took the book over to the umpires—two of them indeed, in tribute to the solemnity of a Semi-Final. One signed cheerfully enough, but the second was deeply worried about something. He examined the book very hard for quite a while before writing a few words of his own and then signing to make the result official and iron-clad.

When the book was returned to me I looked with some interest to see what the problem had been and saw that he had added after my 'Game washed out' the two vital words 'by rain'. Thus some future historian of the game, intent on re-creating the cut and thrust of this epic encounter from the scorebook, will be able to cross-check with the meteorological record and determine that it was indeed an early autumn storm that brought the game to an abrupt end and not a cataclysmic breaking of the banks of the Merri Creek, which flows past the ground. One can never tell how grateful scholars to come may be for such careful documentation.[6]

That the umpire needed so much time for the thought required to come to such a crucial decision might suggest mental processes likely to be caught short in the hurly burly of action, and so it had proved earlier in the game just concluded. I was fielding deep at mid off, and the ball was played straight, beating the bowler (always a strong possibility with Clem Simonetto doing the honours). The striker called for a single, probably on the basis that he had seen me in the field on previous occasions. Even with all three stumps to aim at it was still a considerable surprise to score a direct hit—justification in itself for a raucous appeal, even if the batsman had not been fully stretched.

Up went the umpy's finger to general rejoicing on our part. As I sauntered towards the middle to receive my share of the congratulations (and to hear the verdict of those square of the wicket who thought we'd been more than a bit lucky with this one) I passed the umpire busily re-making the wicket. He volunteered the comment as I passed, perhaps trying to re-assure himself about what, as he reviewed the

---

6   Neither scorebook, however, will reveal the more material fact that the 'C. Price' who opened the bowling for us and was not out when the match came to its premature end was in fact Steve Loney (see Chapter 3).

action in his mind, may have begun to seem like a pretty dodgy decision, 'They've got no idea these young kids—never learned to slide their bat. He was well in but his bat was in the air.'

From my position at the time of impact there was no way I could see whether the batsman had made his ground or not, but one thing I was certain of was the clouds of dust raised by the sliding bat. As I glanced at the considerable furrow he'd left in the bare earth, it did not seem exactly the right moment to point out to the umpire that the hapless runner had done all that was required of him, nor did I, as captain, later feel the incident sufficiently serious to mention in my match report, thereby exposing a well-intentioned gentleman to the relentless and rebarbative scrutiny that might follow such an unkind comment.

Because in every Association, behind the scenes, there is an elaborate apparatus called the Umpires Panel, presided over by an Umpires Advisor who is the *eminence grise* of the whole competition, and is responsible for maintaining the highest standards of integrity among the badge-wearers under his command.

After each game in which official umpires stand, the respective captains are permitted (usually, indeed, required) to submit reports on how they did their job. And let me assure you they do not hold back! The umpire may wield authority on the field, but beware the fury of the spurned suppliant!

The only hint of comic relief in the infinite tedium of Association meetings arose directly from the primal antagonism between umpire and player. One agenda item was devoted to umpires' reports and tribunal verdicts—although if umpires were not officiating, opposing captains snitchy and self-righteous enough to complain about a player wearing red socks or hitting someone over the head with a spare stump could also lodge reports. The reading out of the reports briefly illuminated the spirit that infuses park cricket. 'Abusive language' and 'disputing the umpire's decision' were habitual if predictable themes, but the previous chapter has indicated some of the exciting variations on offer when teams like The Royal Oak and Northern Sportsmen were locked in mortal combat.

After the umpires had said what they thought of us, we got the chance to say what we thought of them. In the majority of cases the captain would take the easy option and tick the box labelled 'Satisfactory', but once moved, with pen in hand, to express themselves at length, they could be venomous. There was a standard formula to be followed, which was, 'We have no complaints about the umpire's performance except . . .' What followed left one bemused about just how defamatory things might have had to become before they constituted a complaint. Mention of physical debility—specifically, blindness—was a sure sign of a beaten team. References to personal hygiene were also demeaning to those who made them. Who can blame an umpy who defers the starching of his jacket until necessity compels? Certainly not someone like myself, who generally could not locate the second sock until it turned up next Saturday morning, still scrunched up in the kit bag along with a half-eaten banana, malodorous boots, the whites, cap, jumper and even (in the old days before modern undergarments) the never-washed jock strap. From our perspective in Naughton's public bar, it was difficult to know how much godliness suffused the Northern and Combined Churches, but I hope it was in more generous supply than cleanliness.

At the Association meetings, however, there was one particular avenue of complaint which I would listen for and seldom be disappointed: 'The umpire generally did a good job, except that he had some problems with the lbw law in the first week, but he was much better the second week.'

A clear sequence of events lay behind this form of words: we bowled first and appealed for everything but he didn't give anyone out; then they bowled and appealed for everything, and he still didn't give anyone out. Perspective is everything in such matters.

I swear that I was present at a meeting where the opposing captains handed in more or less identical reports, except with the weeks reversed.

The umpires' advisor has the responsibility of solemnly considering these crucial pieces of information in order to arrive at an assessment of how well or badly his men have gone about their tasks. What he says to them behind closed doors has never been revealed to those who go about the business of actually playing, so the masonic mysteries of the umpiring fraternity are no part of this history, though some strange politicking must have gone on there. Amongst the scuff and scumble that constitutes the remnants of the club's documentary history—old scorebooks, annual reports, letters from the Council demanding payment for ground hire, chance survivals from the ravages of time—is a tattered set of pages headed Minutes of General Meeting 18/12/89. As NOBs' only meetings took place on Friday evenings and were measured in pots rather than minutes, the paper in question refers to an Association, not a club, meeting.

Somewhere amongst the evening's business there is a record as follows: 'The president asked that umpire J.S−− be removed from the umpiring panel. This umpire has been asked to leave this Association before, and it was the general opinion of the delegates that he is no longer welcome in the Association.'

Who now can remember if we'd ever had the pleasure of Umpire S−−'s company? And who knows quite what he may have done to so offend our good president? Difficult to reconstruct the circumstances at this distance in time—especially since the minutes record NOBs amongst the absentees—no apology either, so there's another ten or fifteen dollars we must have forked out to prolong the financial viability of the Northern and Combined. But then just imagine the weekly sums milked by *persona non grata* Umpire S−− out of the pockets of guileless players fondly imagining themselves to have been under impartial adjudication when in fact being ground between the upper and the nether millstones. Umpire S––'s disappointment at being denied his Saturday outing may have been tempered somewhat by the fact that in December 1989 the Association was within three months of disappearing from the face of cricket, so he may well have survived us to rejoice in a new incarnation, dispensing justice and annoying another set of bureaucrats. But his offences must have been dire to warrant cashiering from a job so few were willing to take up.

As mentioned earlier, it is usually the players themselves who are required to fulfil the umpiring duties in the absence of a qualified official, though one club I played against in the South Suburban Churches comp had an elegant method of bridging the gap. As we sized up an unfamiliar opposition before start of play, one at least of their entourage failed to strike terror into our hearts. Shamblingly unathletic and grossly overweight, there was no obvious role he was equipped to fulfil. However, as he donned the black trousers and the white coat we began to understand his function.

He had gone to the trouble of taking out his umpire's ticket and was therefore qualified to stand in official matches. Not only this, but he had received a dispensation from the executive that, instead of going on the normal roster, he could umpire his own club's game each and every week. This meant of course that they provided two umpires when they were batting and one when we were batting, with the predictable imbalance in decisions, but what aggravated our sense of being comprehensively dudded was that, being fully accredited, he was entitled to be paid for his afternoon's work, and we had to take the hat around to subsidise systematic injustice.

Nothing entrenches a memory more firmly than a sense of personal affront. The reason I recall this match is the solid and reverberating snick onto my pads as I was given out lbw. Walking off the ground, I passed the captain discussing the event with his cover fieldsman and saying, 'Why'd he give that out? You could hear the snick all over the ground.'

Since, I later discovered, the umpire was his own brother, he seemed uniquely well placed to address his question in the appropriate direction. However, in the noblest traditions of the game he decided to accept the umpire's decision without complaint and soldier on regardless.

Back in the team huddle, I was more vehement about the matter, but in view of the fact that the batsman I replaced (who could bat the ears off me) had retired with blood streaming from a severe head wound, and that three or four of the few balls I'd faced had jumped from a length past the eyebrows, it was much better for my close family that I be safely out of there. Even at the time I don't think I was fully persuaded by my own moral outrage. But it's always nice to have someone else to blame, which is, perhaps, the role that the Laws of Cricket always conceived for the umpire.

However, in the vast bulk of park matches, where no such official appears, the immediate problem of finding someone to do the job is solved in the only practical way available. The bowling team requires eleven in the field—and getting a bare eleven together is hard enough without the luxury of a twelfth man—so only the batting side has spare men around to do the umpiring.

They are conscripted by the captain, two by two and usually unwillingly, to trot out to do their six or eight overs. Never once in all the games of park cricket I played, stretching over more than two and a half decades, did I hear a captain enquire even of a totally new player he'd never met before whether he knew anything about the rules. Such knowledge seemed to be surplus to requirements.

Kitted out all in white,[7] there is one saving identification to mark out the square leg umpire from the similarly attired fieldsmen to his left and right—he is leaning on the oldest, shabbiest bat in the club kit, the one no one would think of going out to take strike with. This means that when the batsman turns the ball square of the wicket on the on side he can in an instant recognise that the angularly inclined figure, anchored, as it were, to an ancient willow, is one of us, and calls with confidence for the quick single. Such confidence is well placed, because, however far short of his ground his partner may be, he will not be given out, unless he has tripped over the join in the mats and is lying flat on his face mid-pitch.

It is the responsibility of the square leg umpire to turn down all run out and stumping appeals, and then at the end of the over, in a ritual dear to the heart of all park cricketers, trot half way towards his companion who has been officiating at the bowler's end to hand over the bat which is the symbol of their authority. He then takes up his stance at the new bowler's end in order to deny all lbw appeals and any catches behind the wicket within the radius of first slip.

Despite the fact that normal practice is never to give out anyone in your own team unless at least two stumps have been struck from the ground, everyone in the fielding side is both surprised and resentful at encountering the sort of behaviour in which they themselves colluded only a week before.

Much of the unique flavour of cricket played at this level arises from the predictable collision of views.

A whole career subject to the vagaries of park cricket umpiring should immunise you against a sense of moral indignation as the most blatant dismissals are brushed aside, but it never does. I

---

7   Absurdly, all Associations insist that players acting as umpires must wear regulation gear, exactly the same as the fieldsmen. And they fine the club if someone goes out clad in a style that distinguishes them from the opponents. Official umpires of course wear black trousers, but it is a serious offence for a mere player to do the same. Apparently it falls into the same category as impersonating a policeman.

particularly recall a wild swipe to leg by one of the Thomastown turkey shooters where the deflection was so wide the only doubt was whether keeper or fine leg would take the catch. Somehow the umpire didn't quite see it like that. When the batsman plonked the next two balls over the square leg boundary my sense of being hard done by was considerably aggravated. But this is par for the course in park cricket. Pointless to report such events to the next Association meeting, since the meeting would go on forever if every team who felt they'd been robbed were to put their case to the governing body— which would rightly regard your complaint as prim and sniffy anyway. A more immediate form of rough justice is to pull up a stump and threaten to spear the umpire—an extreme reaction, but by no means unknown.

Even the mildest can be stirred by feelings of injustice, however. Damien Byers was a late recruit for the NOBs. A gentle and judicious man, a graduate student in the Law Faculty, he was in no way blessed with cricketing talent, and equally unconversant with the rough and ready conventions of umpiring at our level of competition. We were playing Fitzroy Salvation Army at Prince's Park, and Damien was fielding at fine leg on the boundary. There was a unanimous appeal for the most patent of snicks to the keeper, and premature congratulation of bowler and catcher as the umpire slowly shook his head.

It always takes thirty seconds or so to throw the ball on the ground, scuff the turf and utter an obscenity before shambling back into position for the next ball.[8] We had gone through this part of the ritual and the bowler was on the way in for the next delivery when I noticed, from mid-off, that what was supposed to be deep fine leg was not only within the catching arc but still on the advance. He was waving

---

8   Those concerned to spread the noble game are perpetually worried about the antics of Test players setting a poor example for juniors. But it is a needless concern: such behaviour is endemic at all levels of the game.

an admonitory finger and, now within vocal range, could be heard exclaiming, 'That's not right, umpire. That's not right. I could hear the snick from down there.'

Though no one on the field had been in a worse position to judge the incident, he walked with the stubborn purpose of those who know the rightness of their cause, and the protest march seemed likely to produce a frontal collision with the umpire

Since we'd all heard the snick, umpire included, this demonstration was unlikely to change anyone's mind. As acting captain, it was my duty to impress upon my overly-earnest colleague that there wasn't much we could do except resume normal fielding positions. That may not be quite the terminology I used at the time, but the general gist is there.

The makeshift umpiring arrangements which are standard for park cricket depend on trust and honesty—qualities not always abundant among those who play as if the proverbial sheepstations are at stake

There were, however, one or two noble souls scattered around— and some of them indeed in our team—who felt that, in the absence of official umpires, it was obligatory to give people out when they were out and to walk when you knew you were out. If you take advantage of a system so liable to abuse eventually there's no system left. Max Radcliffe was one who especially insisted that you had to do the right thing, otherwise there was no point in playing. But even such scruple and years of consistently giving himself out and giving his teammates out (which he enjoyed much more) did not confer blamelessness in the eyes of opponents. Umpiring at the bowler's end one day, Max was the target of volumes of abuse when he turned down an appeal for a catch at the wicket just as the batsman seemed to be heading towards the boundary, accepting the inevitable. Pausing as he saw himself not being given out, he moved back towards the batting crease as the fielding side turned on the offending umpire: 'You've got to give him out—he was walking.'

Max replied, 'If I thought he was out I'd have given him out in the first place. If he wants to give himself out that's up to him.' An entirely proper stance—but completely lost upon our opponents. The batsman's momentary indecision was their certainty. He was out and he knew he was out and so did the umpire and they're all a pack of cheating bastards. This was a depressing but predictable reward for honourable behaviour—another bunch of hoons who are convinced you're a cheat.

My own position was, in principle, the same as Max's—except that sometimes I wasn't quite sure that it wasn't a wandering cicada rather than the ball that had brushed the edge of my bat and so would stand my ground as the Laws of Cricket allow.

The debate about 'walking' must be as old as the game itself. The Poms have a great line in self-righteousness about the sun never setting on the sinking ship, and profess their horror at rude colonials who stand their ground defying the umpire to give them out. There are two sides to every question. When Bill Lawry batted, every umpire knew he wasn't moving unless they told him to go. When they did, he never dissented or showed annoyance, and everyone knew exactly where everyone stood. On the other hand, some of the great English gentlemen of the game who, having spent a lifetime (well, at least an extended boyhood) building up a reputation for walking, come the big game, come the important innings, come the fine snick and the big appeal, are unconcernedly prodding the wicket as the umpire has his sudden second thoughts—'Well, he would have walked if he'd hit it, wouldn't he?' It's not hard to tell who the real cheat is.

But what is reasonable in Test matches with independent officials becomes outright coercion when applied to your own team mates.

Not all opponents, of course, were assiduously dishonest. Some would give decisions as they saw them, and you would strike the occasional walker who would give himself out if he knew he'd snicked it. But it was totally unpredictable who would and who would not play the game fairly. For instance, one learned to be wary of Church teams. The conviction that God is on your side has rarely made anyone behave particularly well towards others.

NOBs, however, while harbouring no delusions about where we stood with the deity, made some effort to do more or less the decent thing in this area of the game, and over the years some of our more regular opponents came to recognise the fact and even to reply in kind. It took quite some time, however, to convince West Lalor of our good faith after our first game against them. With NOBs nine down and one run behind there was a noise that those of us on the boundary line sixty or more yards away thought sounded palpably like a snick and West Lalor were certainly of the same opinion. Johnny Carroll, who was officiating at the bowler's end at the time, has ever since refused to discuss the matter either on or off the record and one has no choice therefore but to respect his discretion in the matter. Though they weren't to know it, West Lalor was doubly unfortunate. If the batting line-up had been properly drawn up, Johnny was a more or less automatic choice as last man in, and therefore should have been occupying the crease rather than handing out the decisions at the moment in question. The final pair added only another two runs, exactly the number required to arouse righteous wrath in our opponents.

Steve Loney also admits to having consciously and deliberately given one decision that fell short of the highest class. This was a season and more before he joined the team, but he came down one Saturday to watch his mate Crossman play. At some stage in the afternoon, probably because no one else could be bothered, he was prevailed upon to go out and do a spell of umpiring. One of the batsmen was Johnny Code, who the year before had been one of Steve's teachers at Northcote High.

Steve recalls that when he stood *in statu pupillari* most of his dealings with Johnny involved, on Johnny's part, a sharp intake of breath between clenched teeth and a vigorous if despairing shake of the head.

As a cricketer, Johnny liked to swing the bat at an off drive, and that was about it. He performed his trademark shot, missing the ball entirely and being carried by his momentum a good foot or so outside his crease. The bails were whipped off and an appeal made to the square leg umpire.

Steve had played quite enough cricket to know the conventions of umpiring—never give your mates out—and in memory of past relations turned down the shout, to the justified annoyance of the fielding team. Johnny knew as well as Steve exactly what had happened, and looked at him with the same sharp breath and the same shake of the head—but neglected to walk, as some might have done in the circumstances.

In spite of occasional aberrations such as these, we gave a lot more out than were ever given to us, and every season the number of NOBs dismissed lbw overwhelmed the number of wickets we took in this fashion. There was even one noteworthy occasion when Peter Horsburgh gave Geoff Crossman out lbw on 99. Though the umpire could not have known the precise score at the time, when he subsequently found out he did nothing but laugh uproariously and invite everyone to admire his flawless and instinctive sense of occasion. In the circumstances we felt it necessary to call on the services of the Club Philosopher in the pub afterwards to rule on such extraordinary behaviour. Professor Doctor Taylor judged that the categorical imperative involved was that charity begins at home, and the guilty party would have to buy his own beer for the night. It wasn't much of a punishment really, since its only effect was to release Horsburgh from any obligation to restrain his rate of consumption to the pace of the slower drinkers in the school.

In another match, the lbw balance threatened to tip decisively in favour of our opponents. Much taken by the radio commentators' use of the phrase 'plumb lbw', Pat O'Connor arrived for the game announcing that he was particularly looking forward to umpiring that day. He had in his pocket the appropriate item from the morning's shopping. Woe betide any batsman subject to an lbw appeal while Pat was officiating. A good joke is worth any amount of unfairness, and Pat was ready at the first smack on the pads to produce a large and succulent blood plum in demonstration of his verdict.

Unfortunately for Pat, the toss went the other way and the opposition batted. He was therefore forced to take the field rather than the umpire's post. At an early point in proceedings, probably in an attempt to win the weekly award for the useless dive of the day, he went sprawling after the ball, forgetting the plum that was still in the right pocket of his trousers. For the rest of the day—and indeed for many washes afterwards—the purple stain of plum juice formed an attractive contrast to his off-whites and the black socks he habitually wore.

Though an unusual umpiring accessory, Pat's plum was not the only extra burden imposed on umpires in our competition. One of the opposing teams had a special requirement. They really only had one player, who bowled at a lively pace and batted like a threshing machine. He was capable of winning a game in very quick time. Though captain of the side, he had one serious defect as a team player, which was that he was a heart surgeon on permanent call. When he walked out to bat he would entrust an electronic device to the umpire to monitor incoming emergencies. This was in the primitive days of mobile communication, before you could take a fax machine and a satellite geographical positioning system out to bat with you. It was just a simple bleeper that was likely to go off at any time, informing the bowlers who were being put to the sword that they were about to enjoy undeserved respite.

We always assured him that, in the circumstances, he was welcome to resume his innings after his return (though the Laws of Cricket did allow us to override the request), but we always hoped, with no malice towards the suffering members of our community, that the emergency would be just serious enough for us to get the rest of the side out before he could rejoin us.

Such readiness to answer the call showed an awareness of his Hippocratic duty to relieve suffering far beyond that displayed by a different medical practitioner with whom I played briefly in another competition.

One of our bowlers made a courageous but ill-timed attempt to cut off a thumping straight drive, dislocating a finger in the process. Strolling casually in from the fine leg boundary to the far wicket, the person best qualified to lend assistance was easily the last of the team to arrive at the scene of pain. Assessment did not take long— we all knew what was wrong even if too squeamish to do what was required—and execution was also brutally swift. Yanking the skewed digit back into alignment, oblivious to the screaming agony of his patient, he muttered more or less to himself, 'That should be all right,' and sauntered back to his fielding position.

Tommy's camaraderie and general team spirit earned him a degree of affection among his colleagues that displayed itself a week or two after the finger incident. Going in to bat late on the second day of the game with the side in a parlous position, it was his job to play for time and hold on for a draw. He took so long getting to the crease, taking block, inspecting the field, waiting for a frolicking dog somewhere over the midwicket boundary that he suggested might scurry round behind the bowler's arm and then patting his bat in the block hole that the rightly indignant bowler raced in and let one go before the new batsman had looked up. The ball took the off-stump out of the ground and, given all the shenanigans preceding it, the official umpire saw no reason to intervene. What's more, no one in the batting side, except the aggrieved striker, was moved to point out that delivery of the ball before the batsman is ready is contrary to the spirit and the letter of the laws of the game—not to mention life-threatening.

Over the next several weeks both stories were enthusiastically re-counted to each new set of opponents, who were thus made vividly aware that whatever they chose to do to Tommy was all right by the rest of us. And no protest was made in the captain's match report of the flagrant breach condoned by our white-coated official.

It was one of those unifying moments, such as only team sports can bring about, where two hostile tribes are brought together and true comradeship is forged. And it is all so simple to achieve, as long as you have a sacrificial victim. There must be one and one only of these—two becomes a faction and the recipe for discord. But as long as there is one person in the team that everyone else knows they dislike more than they could possibly dislike any member of the op-position there is a perfect basis for understanding—apologies given, no offence taken, have another beer, look forward to playing you again next season.

But the internal politics of a cricket team deserves a chapter to itself.

8

Internal Rivalries

Like all sporting teams of a predominantly social character, Naughton's Old Boys were not bound together by delusions of glory or any sense of common purpose, such as a premiership to be won. Comradeship certainly there was, and beer in quantity. But most of all, what kept the team together was a wholehearted enjoyment of the disappointments and humiliations so frequently visited upon one's colleagues, and especially one's best mates.

A wise Frenchman—hard to believe he didn't know something about cricket—once remarked that 'in the misfortunes of our best friends we always find something not entirely displeasing'.

The Cambridge mathematician, G.H. Hardy, who certainly was a keen player and student of the game, grasped its subtle essence: 'Cricket,' he observed, 'is the only game where you are playing against eleven of the other side and ten of your own.' Another one of Hardy's, to which the secret thoughts of every opening batsman return an echo: 'If you are nervous when you go in first, nothing restores your confidence so much as seeing the other man get out.'[1] It is a great tonic to know that, whatever disaster may befall the team from here on, they can't blame *me*.

What Hardy relished in the game was its hypocrisy. Though you take the field as a team, you play alone.

Cricket is perhaps unique among team games in the extent to which individual performance can be distinguished from the overall team result. The scoring system makes it not only possible but inevitable. No full-forward can kick a bag of goals without someone delivering the ball to him, but in cricket, carrying your bat for 50 while the rest of the rabble collapses to 80 all out makes you a being altogether superior to your miserable team mates.

Even baseball—a game of total specialists, where the one thing you're in the team to do can be minutely analysed—still features statistics like sacrifice flies, where you give yourself up to advance a team mate, and runs batted in—where you actually help someone else to score! Not so in cricket.

With one exception, nothing in the mountain of detail recorded in a cricket scorebook has anything to do with teamwork. The exception is that taking a catch or making a stumping actually enhances someone else's bowling average. But park cricket introduces a ruth-

1   G.H. Hardy, *A Mathematician's Apology,* foreword by C.P. Snow, Cambridge University Press, Cambridge, 1979, p. 46.

less levelling factor here to dispel even this faint semblance of team-work.

It being a considerable struggle to get eleven players on the field, very seldom is there someone left over to attend to the score book. As a result, the other team is invited to look after it on your behalf. They of course have no idea who anyone on your side is.

Every change in the bowling is greeted with the raucous cry from the boundary, 'Bowler's name?'—since this is an element they really do need to get right. But who can be bothered enquiring after the identity of an anonymous catcher? Back in the pub after the game everyone who has actually taken a catch that day is most anxious to ensure that his name is entered into what is left of the space after a rude hand has scrawled 'Caught'.[2] Often there are several claimants for the same catch—which suggests something the reverse of team co-operation, more like a fishing competition.

In any case, 'catches taken' has now become a stand-alone statistic and thus a measure of individual prowess, only incidentally a team contribution. And because everyone knows that at the end of the season the tally is going to be topped by the wicket-keeper followed by any half decent first slip, one quickly ignores that statistic—unless one happens to be wicketkeeper or first slip, of course.

As everyone who has played cricket at any level whatsoever knows, a bowler's delight when a fieldsman takes a brilliant catch never equals his disgust when any sort of chance goes down. Or, seen from the bowler's point of view, one is duly grateful when a friend and colleague does what he should, and proportionately disappointed when some rotten mongrel lets the whole team down.

Accordingly, in NOBs scorebook every season no statistic was more carefully kept than one for which the scorebook itself makes

---

2   A researcher from the New Right intent on demonstrating the lamentable standard of public education could do worse than to take a sample from park cricket score books. Calligraphy, spelling and simple arithmetic leave much to be desired.

no provision. The blank inside back cover in our book was devoted exclusively to dropped catches—and we often needed the whole of the space it provided.

Few performances by any team in any competition can have quite matched our opening day of the 1981–82 season. It was a bitter wintry day quite unsuited to gentlemanly relaxation, but not even that and our off-season training regimen (i.e. staying in the bar till stumps every Friday) could excuse dropping 13 catches for the afternoon. Throw in a couple of crook umpiring decisions (no more than we deserved) and that's equivalent to having to get the oppo out two and a half times over. This was another game we lost by a fair margin.

Some of us pleaded extenuating circumstances. The first one I dropped was the next ball after a miscued pull shot which anyone within 20 yards of the wicket could have reached. 'Leave it to me. Leave it to me. I've got the gloves!' cried wicketkeeper Max Radcliffe, as the icy southerly wind curled the ball, with all its savage underspin, towards the chest, straight at the forehead, over the head, leaving Max flat on his back as the batsmen came back for two off a shot that ended about ten yards from the popping crease. Some of us would have appreciated a decent interval so that we could meditate on the richness of the incident, perhaps ask Max to explain some of the finer points of his footwork—certainly to recover our breath. But an irate and inconsiderate bowler steamed in for the next ball before we were properly settled, and a gently ballooning edge to me at second slip went the same way as the previous ball.

Quite rightly this was not regarded as an excuse sufficiently powerful to escape recording on the inside back page. In fact, in the after-match session in the bar that day no one had any dispute about any of the chances that had come his way. But on a normal Saturday nothing was the subject of louder debate — and often quite sincere distress—than whether or not a particular incident fitted into the 'dropped catch' category. 'But I didn't get a hand to it!' the more legalistic would complain. 'That just proves what a slow-arsed nancy you are,' was the usual reply.

From time to time it would come to a vote whether or not something should go down as a genuine missed chance. Never once did the majority agree that the culprit should be excused or the accusation dismissed, and the aggrieved party was usually voting in a minority of one. Whatever our own shortcomings, we expected nothing but the highest standards from our colleagues.

In the days before Velcro found its way into our cricket bags, one particularly admired missed catch occurred through what might be termed 'mechanical failure', though the perpetrator was not spared responsibility. Keeper Radcliffe, rugged up against the chilly wind in a woolly jumper and arms crossed casually behind his back, stood chatting to the slip field. Clem Simonetto was well into his run-up before Max bent into the wicketkeeper's stance—but too late to extricate himself from the emergency that immediately arose. The ball took a healthy edge and deflected at a comfortable catching height just wide of Max's right hip. But the tightening buckle on the back of his right glove had snagged in the woollen jumper, and his hand remained firmly imprisoned behind his back. The best he could manage was to turn and, assuming a stance reminiscent of Napoleon and other great generals of history, watch imperiously as the ball sped away to the distant boundary. Even Clem's patience was somewhat strained on this occasion.

Occasionally a successful catch would be celebrated with as much enthusiasm as a drop—none more so than when Max took a rather good one, at full length in the right glove. The appropriate congratulations were voiced on the ground, but what made this one especially memorable was that Max felt all the regulars in the bar that evening deserved a series of re-enactments to appreciate the glory of the moment. This required moving various hapless drinkers out of the way so that the full dimensions of the dive could be demonstrated.

All this took place in the days when the licensing laws incorporated the absurdity of requiring the floors of public bars to be carpeted. Given the oceans of spillage and worse that rained on them, no publican could prevent them becoming seedy, repellent and unhygienic. The dried beer caked into them and the constant foot traffic produced a harshly abrasive surface.

Max was on perhaps his third repetition of his spectacular feat when he landed rather more heavily and scraped to a halt against the cigarette refuse tray at the foot of the bar. He lost a fair bit of skin off his arm, and after a minor infection set in he experienced a protracted period of pain and discomfort. Little sympathy was extended to his suffering, though the event lived on in popular memory.

Another feature of the game, not necessarily conducive to the overall level of teamwork but regularly celebrated by NOBs, was the 'Useless Dive of the Day' Award (for which Max's *après sport* efforts were a contender). This award had been pioneered by Pat O'Connor, who was very much of the opinion that a game should be analysed in terms of ''ighlights', amongst which he greatly esteemed the sight of a fieldsman spread full length on the turf as the ball sped past his futile grasp.

Pat himself was well known for his endeavours in this area, and usually defended the technique on the grounds that if you made the dive seem sufficiently life-endangering you could convey the impression that you were out of action for quite some time, in which case someone else would have to do the chasing for you.

Second only to the unsuccessful dive, Pat relished the spectacle of run out confusions, preferably with the batsmen stranded either midpitch or both at the same end—anyway, within a bat's length of each other so that mutual recriminations could take on an edge of excitement. It was immaterial to Pat whether it was NOBs or our opponents who were exposed to such embarrassment.

In one of my earliest games for the team, I was the victim of a grotesque error of judgement, when Max Radcliffe hit the ball straight to mid on and called for a single. Honouring my partner's call, I was run out by about half the length of the pitch, the only doubt being whether we'd actually crossed or not. After the event Max was profuse in his apologies and accepted full responsibility for the disaster.

I should have realised that this was an indication I had not yet earned acceptance as a member of the team. When a similar thing happened a few weeks later (although then the fault was largely my own) he was not only loudly abusive of my athletic incompetence, but retracted his previous apology and, pre-emptively, all blame for any future occasion on which I should find myself run out.

A facet of the game in which we took some pride was also perversely an opportunity to enjoy the discomfiture of one's teammates, namely our tendency, when umpiring, to give someone out if he actually was out. Other teams enjoyed a comfort zone in any decision that had to be referred to the umpire. From time to time fielders close to the boundary could hear the recently relieved umpire apologising to the ex-batsman he'd just given out, to the effect that he didn't think he could get away with something quite as obvious as that.

Not so with NOBs. Whoever was umpiring was able to congratulate himself on his scrupulous fairness at the same time as he enjoyed dismissing ignominiously one of his mates. Peter Horsburgh's effort in adjudging Geoff Crossman leg before on 99 has already been mentioned, but Horsburgh figured as victim in his turn. Photographic evidence exists of the look of sheer delight on Dave McGaw's face as he raised the finger to dispatch him in the historic match at Fairfield Park.

Horsburgh had been batting beautifully, as he usually did, hampered only by the necessity of getting up the other end and back if the ball didn't reach the boundary. Eventually, trying to turn a very long one into two, he found himself under such pressure that he was forced to make a dive for the crease. There was never much doubt about the decision, though a fastidious cheat might have argued the clouds of dust raised by such an ample frame thudding to earth had obscured his vision. Other observers compared it to a Panzer division grinding to a halt in the terminal stages of the Battle of the Bulge.

But what the photograph plainly shows is how completely Quick Draw entered into the spirit of the occasion, and how thoroughly he enjoyed the privilege of being able to send the big man on his way after such a memorable effort.

The post-match voting for Most Valuable Player offered another opportunity for exploiting various weaknesses of temperament within the team. Every season the award did manage to be won by someone who arguably was the best player in the side; but as we voted 3, 2 and 1 every week it was by no means the case that our opinion was guided by the value of an individual's contribution to the team performance. If someone had managed to make a conspicuous dill of himself he would usually poll well. For instance, on the occasion of Crossman's Famous Fall he was the unanimous choice as Man of the Match without reference to anything else he had done in the game.

The process of decision was by secret ballot, everyone's scrap of paper being thrown into a cap, followed by a solemn drawing out and recording of votes. It was of course regarded as *infra dig* to vote for yourself on such occasions, but from time to time the accusation was made, and on at least two occasions conclusively proven.

After one game in which Ian Ewing had easily topscored and taken four or five wickets, a hasty whisper went round the bar that we'd give him the three votes, but no one was actually to mention him on their slip of paper. As one after another the votes were read out Ian's consternation grew. Eyes bulging, he stammered in his astonishment and outrage: 'What did *he* do? How come *he* gets three votes?'

By flagrant abuse of the processes of the secret ballot, Ian's own vote was manipulated to be the last one drawn. When it was read out—'3 votes, Ian Ewing'—he knew he'd been sprung, though for some reason he failed to find it quite as funny as the rest of us.

In another match Steve Loney had been the standout performer, and it was pointed out to him with some vigour that every one of the entries had contained the name Loney somewhere in the order so he must have voted for himself. The best he could do in self-defence was to establish that he had given himself only one vote and everyone else had given him three.

Such useless modesty was not the way Bob Speechley approached his cricket. Even before he became captain he always, at his own insistence, batted down the list and bowled irregularly — indeed usually quite reluctantly. But though this looks like self-deprecation, a quite different kind of calculation underpinned the strategy.

Towards the end of the 1989–90 season he dropped the scorebook off with Max and suggested he while away an hour or so by working out the averages for the season. Over their next beer together Max mentioned that Bob himself was within a run or two of heading both batting and bowling averages. 'Yes, that's how I worked it out too,' said Bob. 'I think I know how to handle it.'

So for the last couple of games the closest contenders for the batting honours were promoted to open the innings—a judicious use of their talents, obviously—while Bob continued to provide stability for the tail, occasionally going in as low as number 11. Sometimes he'd bat as high as number 8, but usually on days when we were batting one or two short.

In a side as strapped as we were for players of any real ability, batting that low meant that he would almost certainly be accompanied by partners who might hang on long enough for him to scratch up 8 or 10, but were most unlikely to outlast him. A nice little red ink never does any harm to the average.

One stumbling block to Bob's plans might have been the day when Webbie, batting at number 10, hung on to make 19 not out. But by that time Bob had rattled up 53 in a last-wicket stand of 68. A scoreboard showing a progression from 7/200 to 363 all out suggests something not quite right in the batting order.

At the same time, Bob shrewdly assessed his own inoffensive off breaks as unlikely to trouble well-set batsmen at the top of the order, but they were just the ticket for tail end bunnies.

Through such careful management of team resources Bob was able to head both batting and bowling averages (aggregates were irrelevant, averages win trophies) for the season.

As this was NOBs's (and the NCCCA's) last season of existence, Bob's achievements entitled him to be the perpetual holder of the annual batting and bowling trophies devised and constructed by Quick Draw McGaw, a privilege greatly enhanced by the fact that the trophies went missing years ago—or were perhaps destroyed by someone with the rudiments of aesthetic criticism.

But when it came to intense and enduring rivalry within the team, none of the rest of us came close to Ian Ewing and Steve Loney. Best mates since childhood, they joined the club on the same day and their careers ran in tandem, bound together by nothing so much as their whole-hearted disparagement of each other's endeavours.

A fairly typical moment occurred in a social game against the Black and White Gentlemen's XI, when Steve had the pleasure of umpiring at square leg as Ian sallied forth to a spinner and found himself subject to an appeal for stumping.[3] The appeal was unnecessary, really, since the finger was in the air before the bails hit the ground.

Ian's momentum carried him full circle, the bat thudding to earth inside the crease. He looked at his exultant colleague, then at the bat grounded within the crease, then back at the umpire, exclaiming, 'What the f––– do you think that is, a jam doughnut?'

The force of this persuasive argument was lost on Steve, whose decision was not likely to be swayed even by so inventive a metaphor. Ian returned glowering to the boundary, and when Steve later went in to bat he did so accompanied by a willing volunteer umpire, loudly informing the opposition that any appeal would be favourably considered.

For years Steve was our best bowler, and rightly took the new ball every match—though Ian regularly raised objections to this practice. In one match—and only one fortunately—Steve decided to see how he'd go with off breaks. The ball was clattered to the boundary with such gusto that it must have taken some resolution (aided by possession of the captaincy) to try a second over, which went the same way as the first.

None took greater delight in the spectacle than Ian, hallooing and cheering 'There's another one!' after every ball. Not only did it form the entire subject of his conversation for the evening, for weeks thereafter he would wrench the topic back to this memorable incident, engrossing it in detail in each repetition.

---

3   Stumped in fact by Max Radcliffe, playing for the opposition. He justified this act of treachery on the grounds that he had been playing for the Black and Whites for longer than NOBs had been in existence. This sentimental loyalty to the Collingwood connection should deceive no one, however. All his young life Max was a South Melbourne supporter. Tired of constant floggings, he converted to the Magpies, this event taking place *before* the re-location to Sydney, so he cannot claim the excuse of having been abandoned by his club, and stands revealed as a turncoat. Being born a Collingwood barracker is a misfortune visited on large numbers of people; actually choosing to become one is an act of monumental folly, rightly attended by a lifetime of misery and disillusionment.

And yet, from time to time, Ian himself when thrown the ball would take it into his head to wheel over his own variety of off breaks, quite as innocuous as Steve's. As captain, I found it was no use at all setting a field for medium pacers and insisting he bowl that way if he had decided on the rubbishy off-breaks.

It was fairly inevitable that Steve would become captain at some stage. He was clearly the best sportsman in the side—though this was not a necessary criterion, as my captaincy demonstrates. But when he took over after the 1981–82 season, Ian began immediately to plot his overthrow. For a couple of years the Annual Report was a blizzard of propaganda one way or the other. The anonymous author of the Social Report (not hard to guess who) drew attention to Steve's over-exuberant declaration that he would score a thousand runs for the season, and the subsequent shortfall of about 700. By way of riposte, the Captain's Report mentioned this prediction as seeming like the season's most unattainable boast until 'a certain player' (again one guess would be enough) announced that he thought he had a good chance of knocking off 'a certain barmaid at a certain pub.' There was only one hotel in question, and a quite attractive member of staff at the time. The two predictions proved to be equally inaccurate.

After a couple of seasons roles were reversed, and the retiring captain in his annual report congratulated himself on the prospect of becoming 'a normal member of the team again', a role which he went on to define as 'drinking,[4] whingeing about field placings, getting the sulks because I'm not getting a bowl, sucking up for votes.' As this is a pretty complete description of Ian's demeanour for the previous two seasons one could confidently predict that the new skipper would have all the support his predecessor had enjoyed.

---

4   Nothing in Steve's behaviour had suggested that this was not also an important part of the captain's role.

After NOBs folded up for good and all, Ian and Steve decided on a change of pace and took up lawn bowls. Their choice was heavily influenced by the view, expressed by Steve, that any sport where you can drink while you're playing has a lot going for it. They soon discovered they were in fact both quite good at the game, and more than one club was anxious to secure their services. Steve stayed with his local club at Moonee Ponds, later switching to Preston, but Ian was swayed by the blandishments of Altona, a big-spending club that was intent on swamping the opposition and keen to recruit promising young men ('young' being a flexible category in lawn bowling).

Altona duly carried off several titles, Commonwealth Games gold medals and the like, and Ian progressed to skipper of his rink. But not all has been wine and roses in recent years. In 1999, though unbackable favourites, Altona crashed to defeat, first in its semi-final and then in the preliminary final against Burden Park. A newspaper report of the match was not slow to lay blame and name names:

> After its fightback, Altona just couldn't put in the really big ones evidenced by Ewing's last bowl, 25th-end drive to kill the end. He missed by a long way.
>
> The clash was best summarised at the game's end when one of the Altona players was heard to say, 'no, we didn't deserve to win because we've got too many prima donnas.'[5]

The whole tone of the article was so reminiscent of NOBs in its heyday that, in spite of the by-line, it was difficult to believe the article was not written by Steve Loney.

---

5   *The Sunday Age*, 14 March 1999, 'Sportsunday' section page 23.

A year later disaster befell Altona once again. Reaching the Grand Final, they were again long odds-on for the pennant, only to be skittled by Melbourne, the face of hallowed tradition against the moneyed upstarts. Again the *Sunday Age* invoked Ian's name, this time describing his efforts as 'having a dog of a day'.[6]

Sensitive to the humiliation of our former team-mate, Bob Speechley was immediately on the phone, anxious that full details of the disaster be broadcast to as wide an audience as possible.

Individual rivalries aside, NOBs possessed an indispensable social cement in that—by accident, never by design—we always had one person in the side (and never more than one) who was heartily disliked by everyone else. The social pariah is the necessary catalyst for a sense of identity and solidarity. It has already been recorded that NOBs began with the unanimous blackballing of the person responsible for the club coming into existence. Throughout our history, just often enough to preserve a decent continuity, there was always one of those social unfortunates whom everyone instantly dislikes who somehow managed to insert himself into the team—and, once in, no one in our club ever got dropped, so he was there for as long as he liked to buy his own beer.

Surprisingly, none of these lame dogs was inflicted on the club by Patrick O'Connor, even though Pat was our most ardent recruiter, always on the lookout to dragoon an unwary drinker from his corner of the bar and pitchfork him into tomorrow's game. Allied to this was Pat's total gregariousness and lack of malice. Always one to

6   *The Sunday Age*, 2 April 2000, 'Sport' section page 22.

take people on their own estimation, he was the natural victim of the tedious bar-fly who couldn't find anyone else to put up with him.

I became vividly aware of this during our extended visit to the Leeds Test of 1981, when I imposed mightily on the hospitality of Pat's extended family in Halifax. The match itself ranks high among Australia's sporting disasters, during which two of the nation's finest cricketers (not Pat and me—Marsh and Lillee this time) committed the unbelievable folly of taking a bet on their own team to lose. Events down the years suggest that this was an action even more monumentally idiotic than it seemed at the time.

We should have known from Day One that it would turn out to be a bad experience. Not just the weather, which was distinctly Yorkshire—clouds and spitting rain, with play only intermittently possible. Early in the piece Pat struck up a conversation with a nearby spectator, Richard, who turned out also to be from Melbourne. Rain forced the players from the field for what was going to be a considerable interval, so we repaired to a pub outside the ground, accompanied by our new acquaintance.

After five minutes of Richard's conversation I experienced the sensation of death rapidly approaching. Somewhere in there he was complaining that he hadn't been able to find accommodation in Leeds and would have to catch the train to London at close of play. To my appalled surprise I heard Pat offering bountiful hospitality: 'Dun worry. 'Alifax is only 16 marl away. Broother Tim's on 'olidays an' Jim's staying at 'is place tonnart. There's a spare rum.'

Richard was more than happy to accept. The rain eased shortly afterwards and we returned to Headingley, but by this time Pat had heard enough of Richard's conversation to form an opinion more-or-less identical to mine.

'What 'ave Ah dun? 'ow do Ah get aart o' this?' he said. I suggested a bland lie might be convenient—he'd rung his brother to check if it was OK and found out they were coming home a day early, or something to that effect. To someone of Pat's honesty, duplicity does not come easy, and he was consumed with remorse at his own generosity, but convinced of the necessity of execution.

What he said to Richard by way of excuse I never knew, but the connection was severed. Or so it seemed. Two days later as we relaxed on the northern terrace[7] of the ground, the game was interrupted for a considerable period as players and umpires waved their arms with increasing frustration at some ignorant fool standing straight behind the bowler's arm, in the area where the white painted seats and fences served in place of the absent sightscreen. With no one at all for thirty metres either side of him, there was no mistaking who the offending presence was, but the intruder himself, dancing around to try to get the best camera angle, remained oblivious of the fact that the attention of the entire ground—and television screens in the dark reaches of the Australian night—were focused exclusively on him. They could have had an extra drinks break in the time it took to move him on, but long before then Pat had exclaimed in aghast tones, 'Bluddy 'ell, it's Richard!'

Forced from his vantage point, Richard trekked along the public concourse[8] in our direction. Pat ducked his head pretending to be searching among the sandwiches for something or other, hoping the crowd was dense enough to offer camouflage, but all in vain. Waving his hand with a cheery greeting, the object of the wrath and contempt of the whole Yorkshire crowd was with us again.

---

7   To describe any part of the Headingley Cricket Ground as a terrace suggests a Mediterranean ambience rather at odds with the actualities of the ground.
8   Again a word suggestive of an opulence not necessarily to be found at Headingley.

I met up with Pat a couple more times during that long and pleasant (cricket and Richard excepted) English summer. Come the Old Trafford Test, where collective insanity and Ian Botham again descended upon Kim Hughes's gallant boys, Patrick had a story to tell me that shook him to the bones. He'd been on the train from Leeds to London — a longish trip in a small island — and he and Pip decided to visit the buffet in search of pies or beer or whatever might sustain them on the journey, when Patrick made an abrupt turn mid-carriage, forcing Pip back the way they had come. 'Ah daren't go,' he said. 'Richard's there.'

Hastily snatching their bags from their seats, they fled to the end seat in the end carriage, where Pat huddled in a corner, vividly aware of the linear nature of railway carriages and the impossibility of evading a determined pursuit. When the train reached London, Pat was by a long way the last to leave.

The Oval Test is the sentimental farewell to an English summer. Pat had made long-distance arrangements for seats on the Saturday, and we arranged to meet, along with another NOB then resident in London, Graeme Mulvey—according to his school coach a better cricketer than Yallop, who was to do his stuff before us that very day. A bumper crowd on the Friday, with which the turnstiles could barely cope, made the authorities turn to a peculiarly English expedient. They closed all the gates except one and made everyone join a very, very long queue stretching more than half way around the ground. I witnessed members of the Surrey County Cricket Club shaking their fists in the faces of policemen and shouting, 'I've been a member here for thirty-five years and I've never been treated like this!'[9] Half the crowd didn't get in before the lunch break.

---

9   The English are proud of their public orderliness, as exemplified by their willingness to join a queue. My experience at several cricket grounds was that instead of joining a queue fifty yards long, you could walk down to where they were actually selling the beer and find that the queue was for the first selling station, and that there were four other willing attendants standing around with nothing to do.

Once, an emergency gate opened to allow an ambulance out (were there casulaties so early in the day?) and a great surge of English middle-class law-breakers pressed through the gap, anxious to collide with the thin blue line of law officers. But this was, after all, the greatest English summer of riots for a century or so, and all very instructive to a son of the convicts.

By the time we got inside the ground, play was well advanced, but as we shuffled past annoyed English knees and settled on our seats we were greeted by a far too familiar voice from immediately behind us. 'Hello Pat, hello Jim. Did you know Carlton finished top of the ladder?'

Much as I would have been pleased in normal circumstances to hear of the success of my football team half a world away, the prospect of another day with Richard breathing down the neck was enough to strike despair into the hearts of all who had made his acquaintance. It was an all-ticket affair, so seats were prescribed, which severely limited the chances of escape.

'We've got to find somewhere,' I muttered to Pat, and bolted past the same sets of English knees in search of vacant seats to which we could flee. When I came back with news of a set of seats unlikely to be filled, Pat made a grrateful retreat, but Graeme Mulvey, who had not had the pleasure of Richard's conversation at Leeds, was in no greay hurry to move. Half an hour later, ashen faced, he arrived at our new vantage point. 'I see what you mean!' he exclaimed.

We must have managed to conceal Naughton's Hotel and NOBs Cricket Club from Richard, or I am sure he would have been among us with a vengeance. But he was there in spirit anyway, because the hide of the rhinoceros is the common characteristic of such types.

There was one eager recruit (it would be invidious to use actual names) who stuck around, seemingly oblivious to any insult. Ian Ewing in particular treated him to every kind of rudeness that could be imagined, to which he unfailingly responded with a sort of daft cheerfulness that was itself perhaps his most annoying characteristic. In speculating, in his absence, about what appeared to be a remarkable degree of forbearance, someone offered the suggestion that perhaps he didn't realise he was being insulted. Everyone had behaved like that to him all his life and he thought it was just normal.

One of our number was able to report having been present at a dinner party where the host had conspicuously filled everyone's glass except one. Our absent friend had shown no sign of recognising the snub, but had simply picked up the bottle and helped himself, in exactly the same way he drank everyone else's beer without feeling the necessity of repaying the favour.

One at least of the objects of common disdain was actually quite a good player, but so given to letting you know just how good he was, and so zealously intent on victory that we could almost have mistaken him for one of the opposition. He even took things to the ridiculous extreme of getting stroppy with Clem Simonetto for dropping a particularly easy catch off his bowling—well, not so much dropping as failing to make any movement towards the ball as it looped past. Clem very reasonably responded to the stream of criticism by saying, 'Just go and ask the skipper what the hell he was doing putting me at second slip.' Complaining that Clem was a bit slack in the field meant you'd missed the point entirely and were playing for the wrong team.

In the end I suppose, there is only one way of ensuring a significant degree of popularity in a team whose most important activities take place off the field, which is to be a butcher by trade. Only once have I played in a side containing such an estimable character, one indeed who rejoiced in the remarkably appropriate name of Killingbeck. As Christmas approached—and with it discussion of such functions as a club barbecue—no one was more assured of his place in the side than Charlie, and a chaffbag of chops and sausages was sufficient to make us all agree with the wisdom of our selection policy.

9

Turf Competitions of Another Kind

In every park cricket team, there is one player who will unfailingly turn up with a transistor radio and the form guide.

When no race is actually in progress he is good-natured enough to lend the tranny (though low in the battery and difficult to tune with any precision) to someone who might want to listen to the Test Match—though he finds it difficult to understand why anyone would employ it for a purpose so remote from his own interests. For a few moments at least the nasal excitement of large beasts in motion and larger sums of money changing hands is replaced by the more cultured accents of a Christopher Martin-Jenkins, on loan from the BBC, or Launceston's own Tim Lane. But woe betide any hapless borrower unfamiliar with the starting times at Warwick Farm or Morphettville who does not restore it to its rightful function in time for its owner to trace the familiar pattern of declining fortune.

So evenly is this obsession spread through the ranks that at some point in the afternoon on every park cricket ground across the city someone in the fielding side will turn to the point on the boundary where the batting team is congregated, cup his hands and call out, 'What won the fourth at Sandown?' And there is always someone in possession of this arcane piece of information and thus able to satisfy the applicant.

This enthusiast is by no means the only person in the side interested in horse racing, but he is usually the scruffiest, having been cleaned out by the bookies more often than anyone else. He is also one of those hapless souls who appear, as it were, to be there against their own will, being much more interested in Flemington or Moonee Valley than in any cricket match, yet drawn by some higher power to enact the same farce every Saturday afternoon. It is not unknown for such individuals to barrack for Collingwood.

Unmistakably, this was the role fulfilled in NOBs by Clem Simonetto.

Perhaps it was a fundamental mistake that Clem should have tumbled into a cricket team in the first place. Though by temperament a most clubbable man, neither nature nor tradition seemed to have marked Clem out for this particular pastime. His undiluted Italian heritage did not provide any immediate link with the game and a general flailing lack of co-ordination did not promise well either. Clem was, however, a stalwart. His gangling frame gave him a reasonable turn of pace for our grade of cricket, and somewhere or other he had picked up enough of the rudiments of line and length to be our most dependable bowler.

For several seasons, Clem's bowling action—a combination of praying mantis and whirling dervish—was a distinctive sight in the lower reaches of the Northern and Combined Churches Cricket Association. In his later years, his unusual method of propelling the ball was accented, as the elastic grew slack and buttons popped, by an involuntary grasping at the midsection just after the delivery stride in order to prevent final disaster befalling his ageing and only pair of whites.The brown belt, a particularly admired item of Clem's attire, came to his rescue and temporarily extended his career. Though scarcely regulation gear and thus rendering the team liable to a fine every time he took the field, Clem took solace in the words of Club Founder Pat O'Connor to the effect that 'You needn't take that all-white thing too literally'—as indeed Pat's own characteristic black socks bore witness.

Clem was never observed by anyone to wear a new item of clothing, so his career was finally brought to an end not by the back injuries sustained by more serious fast bowlers but by wear and tear to the flannels. All in all Clem could be said to have been a walking example of life after the bookies have got their hooks in.

Trousers were not the only item of equipment with which Clem experienced difficulty. The academic horn-rims, ill-suited to the cricket field in any case, suffered terminal damage in a dramatic incident late one Friday training session. After a few sherberts, Clem's Mediterranean temperament is apt to display itself in extravagant and not always controlled gestures. Clem was in full training at the time, and was making a vigorous point almost certainly connected with horseracing when a flailing arm made contact with the spectacles, knocking them from the bridge of the nose clean across the bar. His judgement of length was always impeccable, and the specs hit the floor a fraction of a second before the ponderous foot of bar manager and Club Patron Adrian Keeley, with the full force of twenty stone and more upon it. In consequence, Clem's batting was even more unreliable than usual until a replacement pair could be found.

Clem's batting is a subject too painful to dwell on for any length of time, so we will pass over it in silence.

When I was captain I used to bowl Clem all afternoon, which served two purposes: he bowled better than any one else in the side and it removed a weak link in the field, given that he had the width of three stumps to add to his size 14's to stop a straight drive.

He wasn't much good for anything else.

It is often said of a bowler 'fields well off his own bowling.' This bespeaks a certain meanness of spirit, someone so anxious about his own figures that he puts in a special effort to cut off a stroke or pick up a half chance. No one could accuse Clem of such niggardliness. Once he'd let go of the ball, that was it. From there on everything was in the lap of the gods or the even less reliable hands of his fieldsmen. The one occasion he is remembered as having taken a caught and bowled, it was greeted with a flood of congratulations from his teammates. The bemused batsman must have wondered why such a regulation catch should provoke such a degree of enthusiasm.

One of the more ridiculous aspects of the competition was that Clem acquired over a time a fearsome reputation among the more timid of our opponents. It was a source of amusement to NOBs to hear relieved whispers in the ranks of the oppo that 'the Big Fella isn't playing this time.' It was evidence of Clem's genial nature that he was temperamentally incapable of putting the ball around the ears of even the most annoying rabbit. Either that, or the fact that the bouncer takes just that bit more effort to bowl.

In all respects other than his batting, Clem was a master of timing. Each Saturday as start of play approached a quick head count would tally up to ten, and nervous glances would be cast towards the cemetery on our eastern boundary. Unfailingly we would see the lofty and angular figure of Clem Simonetto sloping and dipping between the tombstones in his unique method of locomotion, always in time to take the first over, never quite soon enough to help lay out the mats and plant the flags.

When the club held a reunion in May 1999 we'd more or less given up on Clem after some hours of convivials as we sat down to eat. At this precise moment Clem appeared, walked the length of the dining room to where Horsburgh was sitting at the head of the table and said, 'I think this is yours.' It was an elegantly wrapped parcel that could have been mistaken for a generous serve of Baci chocolates, but was in fact a pewter drinking mug inscribed to memorialise a Horsburgh century scored in 1984. Fifteen years after the event, but Clem could not have choreographed the presentation with more aplomb.

One incident that throws into sharp relief Clem's enthusiastic love of life was the year he took off work—and off playing for NOBs as well. The much-travelled Clem (he is recorded as having once been to Sydney to attend a race meeting) had decided against the usual OS trip, and his exact plans were not known to all the company. Shortly before his withdrawal from the employment pool, Biddo asked him in the bar one night what he was going to do on his year off, to which Clem responded succinctly, 'Stay in bed.'

In fact what Clem had planned for his sabbatical was a determined assault on the bookmakers of Australia—with the odds heavily where they always are. His obsession with the form guide took on new dimensions, and each small success was carefully nurtured against the inevitable turning of the wheel.

Much to general amazement, at the end of his allotted span Clem still had a bankroll, and decided to extend his leave without pay until economic necessity drove him back into the embrace of the Education Department. In time all good things must come to an end, and Clem's good things became fewer and further between until he announced his retirement from Caulfield, Flemington etc. and rejoined us on a regular basis for his Saturday afternoon purgatory.

Clem though never quite enjoyed his second stint as much as his first. 'When I left for my year punting,' he explained, 'we were all quite happy to lose, but when I came back there were blokes keen to win.' One of them, as recorded elsewhere, was so over-zealous as to take Clem to task for dropping a catch—an infallible sign of having failed to enter into the spirit of things.

This particular match was a Semi-Final, and therefore of importance to some at least among us. In the end we lost because Mick Cushen dropped a catch with nine wickets down and NOBs 4 in front, but the earlier indiscretion had been a useful contribution to the final result.

It had been an agonising afternoon all round for Clem. A Grand Final berth would mean that the second weekend in March was booked up, preventing attendance at both the Newmarket Handicap on Saturday and the Australia Cup on the Labour Day holiday on Monday.

NOBs made a respectable 210, but for a while that looked like not nearly enough. Things became more dubious, however, as the batting crumbled from 3/130 to 8/180. Somewhere in there came the moment when the ball wafted slowly wide of second slip with Clem not having moved from his stance.

It would be entirely wrong to suspect that divided loyalties led to a deliberate missed chance. No one who has seen Clem in the field could have any difficulty with the concept of him dropping a slips catch. It is far more difficult to believe he could ever catch anything there than that he would be capable of such perfidy.

As the ninth wicket pair hung on precariously another possibility suggested itself to Clem: "What if the skipper thinks of bringing me back on?"

When the match had finally been lost, he did ask Ian Ewing if the thought of a bowling change had crossed his mind, but Ian showed he was true captaincy material by saying, 'No, Clem, you'd already done all the bowling you were going to do.' A pity really, as Clem is convinced that just one over from him would have put the result beyond doubt.

Australian sporting tradition is shot through with stories about champion players who are actually more interested in the result of a horse race than in the game they are personally contesting. Sheffield Shield matches would take an unscheduled drinks break at 2.40 p.m. on Melbourne Cup day. Keith Miller would feel the twinge of a hamstring just moments before the start of race in which he had taken an interest. Several current stars are notorious. Clem was living proof that you don't need to be a champion to have your mind elsewhere. One Caulfield Cup Day Clem was fielding, as usual, at deep fine leg at about the time his finely honed instincts told him the Cup was due to be run. The members of the batting side not actually engaged in the centre were grouped on the third man boundary, perhaps sixty yards from where Clem found himself. As was entirely predictable, one of them had a transistor radio quite as tinny and reedy as Clem's own. From a distance he could hear the distinctive tones of Bert Bryant, but couldn't quite make out what was being said. With each succeeding ball, prompted by the need to satisfy natural curiosity, Clem edged closer and closer.

The captain usually selects the two greatest lumberers in the team for fine leg and third man, so the latter position was Geoff Crossman's by right. He had a financial interest in the race quite as significant as Clem's own, so had no inclination to change places with him. By the end of the over, we had two fieldsmen side by side on the third man fence, neither of them watching the play. They remained there until the race was over.

In such circumstances it was sometimes difficult for the team's tactical requirements to be met by the resources available to the captain.

It is hard to imagine cricket being played at any level in Australia without horseracing being somewhere near the forefront of several minds, so that even those like the present writer with not a skerrick of interest cannot entirely escape the infection.

The notoriously fickle weather of Melboune's spring profoundly influences the character of cricket in the state. One consequence is that the Victorian Sheffield Shield team goes into its early encounters decidedly underdone compared to the Banana Benders or the Sandgropers. (We still have a head start on Tassie, however.) Another is that for humble toilers at the lower and lowest levels, the hours of emptiness brought about by rain interruptions and complete wash-outs are filled by the mysteries of odds and the tic tac of the betting ring, for the start of each cricket season coincides with the early preliminaries of the Melbourne Spring Racing Carnival.

Confused recollection insists that it always rained on Caulfield Cup day. Certainly two years in a row (which is enough to constitute a minor tradition) play was washed out without a ball bowled—which means, of course, a whole afternoon in the pub.

This unexpected leisure is whiled away watching the races on the telly. To spice up the interest, there's a sweep on each and every race. Not the sort of sweep where you all dob in and horses are drawn from the hat, because that would be fair and give some chance to everyone. Instead, for two bob you can back the horse of your choice, provided someone hasn't got in before you.

This system is of course set up and administered by those with an interest in the sport to start with, and has an inevitable consequence, which is that the bunnies like myself, who don't know the name of a single horse engaged, have to borrow a form guide from one of the keener aficionados. By the time you can get hold of one, the eyes have been picked out of the field, and short of a smokey coming in at 60 to 1, all you're doing is subsidising someone else's drinking for the afternoon.

Horsburgh and Radcliffe were known to revel in these conditions— always being good performers in the heavy going, and never reluctant to take a mug's money off him. Under such conditions much of a person's deeper, underlying character is revealed. It was for instance on one of these occasions that Ian Ewing showed himself to be one of the rare souls for whom every advertising executive spends his life searching—a sensitive index of credulity, the lowest common denominator at which every spiv campaign should be pitched.

As usual, the races were interspersed with a blizzard of commercials, in one of which one of the fast food chains was pushing a super special, before they wisely abandoned it as a market flop. It was called a Double Double, and the ads were commensurately overstated.

His attention riveted by the sound and fury of the advertising, Ian exclaimed aloud to the whole of the bar in tones of wonder and infatuation: 'A Double Double! I've got to have one of them!'

On the instant he raced to his car. Unaware of the exact location of the nearest franchise of this particular brand, he seems to have spent some time searching the neighbourhood, but about half an hour later he returned with not one but two (or perhaps, double doubled, that makes eight) of the revolting concoctions.

Adverse comments were passed by his companions about the appearance of these items. I don't know whether he started on the second, but he certainly didn't finish it. No one offered to help him out. Even Ian felt he been dudded on this particular promotion.

Despite this check to his boyish enthusiasm, nothing in his subsequent behaviour showed that he had grown in wisdom as a result.

Though he sometimes carried a crumpled copy of the racing page in his back pocket, the fact that Ian was prepared to abandon the races for half an hour in search of double delights showed that he was not amongst those sterner souls who have committed their mental energies to the turf and their salaries to the enrichment of sharp men wearing snappy hats.

The hat is of course the *sine qua non* of racing, and Naughton's public bar was particularly fortunate in that Leo, one of the regulars, sported an array of hats which conveyed the authentic aura of early morning track work (doubtful that Leo ever got up to watch) and betting plunges by those in the know (impossible to tell if Leo ever was). Leo always bought the very smallest beers Simon served, which he would hold an inch or so below his chin as, head lowered, he discussed in confiding tones his assessment of whatever was going around next Saturday. Careless talk costs lives, and Leo was never one to spill too much—either of his minute beer, or of any inside information he might have had. Though short on specific tips there was one general point of principle that Leo was given to repeating with a frequency and reverence that surely must have had their origin in one or two successful speculations in Leo's sporting past. His unusual way of accenting the name of his hero lent emphasis and urgency to his advice: 'Never you mind about that Gweorge Hanlon— he knows how to train a racehorse does Gweorge Hanlon.'

The biggest win of Leo's punting career may indeed have been courtesy of George Hanlon, but owed little to the training schedule. It had an authentic flavour, however, which suggests why Leo should have found himself at home in the company of such a mob of no-hopers as NOBs were. Names and dates that give circumstantial detail to the story are missing, and Leo, alas, is no longer around to ask, but he had laid down a fair sum on a horse in the Grand National at Flemington. The horse had no reputation at all for speed, but was a very steady jumper. Leo no doubt was counting on the rest of the field coming to grief before the final sprint for home. The length of the odds was commensurate with this possibility.

Unfortunately, after the required two circuits of the steeplechase course there was still a sizeable bunch contesting the lead and Leo's horse was stone motherless and a furlong off the pace. At this point a kindly fate intervened, as the leading jockey missed the changeover from the steeplechase onto the course proper. The whole bunch followed.

Leo's horse was so far behind as to have no idea of what had happened up ahead and no chance of being misled by the errors of others. The jockey successfully negotiated the changeover while the rest of the field was still trying to pull up and turn around to come back. It was a stroke of fortune that Leo never forgot and never tired of recounting.

But Leo's place in NOBs' folklore is intimately related to the hat, for it was on the occasion of the drawing of our first chook raffle that we prevailed on him to allow us to make use of the hat to perform the essential function. Though he was most reluctant to part with it, he recognised the merits of the cause and it was the first time anyone present had seen him bare headed—and totally bald.

Thereafter we never drew a raffle without making sure beforehand that Leo would be in the bar, and despite a reflexive 'No, no, no' he never refused us the use of the hat.

Leo was a great discusser of racehorses but not much of a divulger of information. Just occasionally, however, word would filter into the bar and find its way to those who had need of it. One morning not long before Cup Day in 1983, a few of the regulars/desperates— those lined up when the doors open—were chewing over the hair of the dog and the merits of the various runners, opinion as always dressed as certainty. At that early stage of the day it was a quiet and sparsely populated bar. Everyone had had his say, except the young kid sitting at the end of the bar nursing a lemon squash. One of the locals turned to include him in the conversation and asked if he had something to offer.

'Kiwi,' he said, apparently unaware of how presumptuous it is of a mere stripling to have so definite an opinion in the company of grown men.

'Why do you reckon that?'

'Well, he's the best horse in New Zealand and he's carrying two kilos under weight for age.'

'How do you know that?'

'I'm riding him.'

This was the young Jim Cassidy, billeted in a motel up the road, just stopping off for a squash after early track work. The morning shift passed on the word to the lunch time drinkers, some of whom were still there when the evening crowd began to arrive. Many regulars of the public bar, several NOBs amongst them, were well and truly on the horse by Tuesday afternoon. It was one of the classic Melbourne Cups, and as the horses turned for home those with their money on Kiwi were loudly exclaiming, 'Why did I back that bloody dog? He's gone and—oh!—won it.'

Though never officially proclaimed a life member of NOBs (no one ever was, a sad oversight) Jim Cassidy is nevertheless enshrined as a team hero.

Not so Jerker McCafferey. As recorded elsewhere, Jerker had carved out a modest reputation with the NOBs when he deserted us to become the vet in attendance at Moonee Valley Racecourse. His specialist skills were much in demand, and in 1993 the connections of a horse called Vintage Crop paid his fares to go to Ireland and supervise the transport here of the eventual Cup winner. It is reported that, having had occasion to witness the beast at the closest of quarters, he laid a sum of money down on his own account, but didn't pass the word on to his old mates.

Similarly Horsburgh. A member of a notable Australian racing family, Peter Horsburgh had turf in his veins. Only a couple of years after NOBs folded up for good a champion sprinter named Hareeba carried all before it for several seasons, winning large and publicly announced prizes for its owners and incalculable sums for those who were given a whisper. 'Owned,' the racing pages always said, 'by the Horsburgh family.' A simple phone call was all that was needed, but he never managed to get in touch.

But even when information did sneak through, the result wasn't necessarily a clean collect. One pre-match warm-up session in the bar, Legs Latta arrived and asked casually (as is his wont) if anyone fancied a bet on a pretty good thing that afternoon. Immediate interest was shown. The tip was that a horse called Megan Lass was a shoe-in. Legs provided much circumstantial detail to support his case. Not much was known about the horse, but he had a mate with a mate at the stable. The filly always went well first up after a spell, which meant no one had had time to take a line through the form. A holding track just suited her style of going, and so on, with more the mug punters didn't understand.

It all seemed very convincing, and various team members tossed into the pot—each according to his ability and several according to their perceived needs, amounting to a tidy sum in the end. One car was delegated to make a minor detour on the way to the game, in order to stop off at the most convenient TAB to lay the wager on behalf of us all.

By good luck we were batting at the time the race started, so even on Clem's reedy and rusty transistor we were able to follow progress. Megan Lass romped in—and when they gave the TAB odds, $8.50 for every 50 cent unit invested, joy was unconfined.

The winning ticket was redeemed on the way back to the pub, and the evening consisted of what used to be called a spree. Quietly satisfied with the way the afternoon had worked out, and patron of our exuberance, was Legs Latta. Legs himself had not slung any money in to the team's TAB whip-round because, as he said, 'My money's going on at the course.'

News reports included mention of a betting plunge that had massacred the bookies, and Legs enjoyed the knowledge of having for once been where the smart money was.

Next time we saw him his mood was less genial. The source of his information was also the person he had entrusted with a significant sum of money to be invested on the horse. His mate (or ex-mate by now) was so agog with the excitement of having been part of a betting coup that he couldn't resist telling the story—how the syndicate had struck on a pre-arranged signal, taking the odds before any of the bookies got a whiff of what was going on, but at the same time apologising that 'Unfortunately, Legs, I didn't get a chance to put yours on so you can have your money back'—an explanation Legs accepted with all the sincerity with which it was offered.

For the rest of its quite successful racing career we followed Megan Lass's fortunes with interest, but thereafter without the assistance of one useful source of information.

Legs could at least claim to have learned a valuable lesson to do with money and friendship, but it is not characteristic of the true gambler to learn lessons of any kind, no matter the scale of the disappointment. A case in point is Patrick O'Connor, who has never ceased to lament the occasion when he failed to make his fortune, though as it happens horseracing was not involved.

The present writer was privileged to be with him at the time, which was the Headingly Test of 1981, perhaps the most famous loss in cricketing history. Patrick and I saw almost every ball bowled in this depressing encounter.

It was my first experience of England, and happened to coincide with a trip home by Pat to introduce his lovely wife Pip to his family. It was arranged that I arrive in Halifax in time for the Test Match only 16 miles away in Leeds.

Australia, batting first, declared when they passed 400, and from there on had the match by the throat. England collapsed and, following on, lost their seventh wicket still almost 100 runs behind. It was around this point in proceedings that after a tour of the ground Pat arrived back to where we were all sitting, announcing in tones of amazement, 'You'll never guess what they're offering in the betting tent—England at 500/1!'

Since the outcome was a lay-down misere, Pat had resisted the impulse to put a few quid on the underdog. We were not to know at the time that two of Australia's most famous players had also seen the odds and decided to have a piece of the action. While no one would suggest it influenced their later play, it was an act of such monumental stupidity as to make NOBs look like a model of decorum and gentlemanly propriety. It also coincided with the most remarkable change of fortune. With inspiration born of despair, Botham teed off at everything. In about an hour he and Dilley had put on over a hundred for the eighth wicket.

In all of this Kim Hughes showed his flair as captain by simply rotating the same three fast bowlers. Although they were the ones who had done all the damage up to now, Botham was taking fifteen an over from them, and no one else could have done much worse. When they finally got Dilley out, in came Chris Old, known throughout the world as a big hitter of slow trundlers but easy pickings for anyone above medium pace. The three quicks were completely knackered by this time, so on came the spinner, to Old's great delectation.

One has a certain sympathy here for Hughes' plight, since the only spinner available to him was Ray Bright, but surely just the faintest experiment by way of a bowling change might have helped. What happened in Australia's second innings scarcely bears thinking about. The middle order of Hughes, Yallop and Border did not manage a single run between them.

After each of the first four days of the game, I had been voluble in the West End pub in Halifax, Pat's brother's local, about the quality of English cricket, and especially Bob Willis. Willis, I maintained, was an embarrassment to his mother and should retire immediately leaving the twelfth man to perform any fielding duties that might be required, since both his bowling and his batting were an impediment to the England cause.

It had already been arranged that at the end of the game I should catch the London train direct from Leeds rather than return to Halifax for another night. So after Willis took 8 for 43 and Australia disappeared down the gurgler, the West End bar that night was full of locals looking in vain for the little Aussie bleeder who'd been so free with his opinions. Two years later, on my next visit, some of them were still waiting, anxious to resume the conversation.

My salutary lesson from the game was not to push hospitality too far and that a strategic withdrawal always beats sticking to your guns. Patrick, however, remains to this day haunted by the thought of the missed 500/1. He has by now convinced himself that he was on the verge of laying down a large sum of money, and only momentary inattention prevented him from making his fortune. Every time we meet it comes up in the conversation, and the wistful look of one who is destined to make a very significant miscalculation comes over him. All a bookie somewhere needs to do is offer 500/1 on some impossibility, and Pat will mortgage the house.

10

Extracurricular

Park cricket is a term that refers to a regular competition, not to the myriad scratch games played under relaxed rules, usually on a Sunday arvo when formal competitions are not taking place. In such games drinking (absolutely forbidden in Church competitions) is not only permitted but virtually compulsory.

Although NOBs was assembled for a far more earnest level of competition, a club of our character and temperament naturally found itself at home in the milieu of social cricket, and every season two or three games of this kind were organised—although given the way we played in even our most important matches, we were not really in need of light relief. Relaxed rules are one advantage of social cricket. Another, which especially appealed to players like me, was that our performances improved markedly when the opposition wasn't trying too hard, and was probably half-shot anyway.

A normal practice in social cricket, to even out the huge disparities of talent, is that batsmen must retire after scoring 30 or 35; everyone bowls (three overs maximum) and run ups are limited to five paces. Often there is a rule prohibiting ducks, though even such benign intentions can create difficulties.

In my first year in Melbourne I was invited to play in a social game Bolshie enough to include the odd Labor parliamentarian; this was almost back in the Menzies era, when the Cold War still raged. One of these elected luminaries, a future Minister of the Crown and Hero of the People's Republic, had already carved out for himself such a reputation for athleticism that someone had constructed for him a bat fully two feet wide. With the aid of this enormous paddle not even he could miss the lollipops served up to him, but the best he could manage was to scoop them all gently to me fielding about four yards in front of him. I must have caught him at least six times before he eventually waddled through for the statutory run that meant we were allowed to get him out.

After this performance, the directors of this annual event rejigged the rules so that three times out was sufficient. The next year I stumped a famous playwright twice, but it was the dolly catch to cover that actually dismissed him.

A more-or-less regular game (that is to say, at least two years running with every intention of continuing the practice) took place against the Black and White Gentlemen's XI, a group of Collingwood supporters plus assorted hangers-on, which frequently participated in such encounters.

It was not one of the agreed rules of our games with the Black and Whites that batsmen be spared the ignominy of scoring a duck, which had unfortunate consequences for Club Founder Pat O'Connor. He had his stumps disturbed while still on the dreaded zero, and returned to the boundary shaking his head in disbelief, exclaiming in his broad Yorkshire accent, 'Ah 'ad it coompleetly coovered.' Steve Loney was quick to offer a word of consolation, telling him, 'Never mind, Pat. You were due for a failure.' In view of the fact that Pat's previous three innings had all resulted in an identical score, that seemed a very accurate review.

Thereafter, for some seasons, whenever one of our number was bowled neck and crop, two or three onlookers could be heard to mutter 'coompleetly coovered' in appreciation of the effort.[1]

From time to time a game was set up between NOBs, who were at least a minimally organised collection of pisspots, and a totally disorganised motley culled from the remainder of the public bar. The two teams could easily be told apart in the field, since NOBs were required to have something resembling regulation gear to play in, whereas the scratch team from the bar would turn out in a seedy but colourful array of casual clothing, and in numbers sufficient to fill the outer at the MCG. In one game they were victorious with a mere 17 wickets down—plus a few retired along the way.

There was a particular hazard attending our performances in these games, since anyone so bold as to be part of an actual team is, at least implicitly, claiming to have some skill at the game, and the ignominy

---

1   Only after I had played three or four games for the Black and Whites did I discover that my debut game had been preceded by an emergency meeting of the team's organising committee to discuss my acceptability. They had discovered my allegiance to the Carlton Football Club, and although barrackers for Geelong, Fitzroy, St Kilda and even Essendon were tolerated, it was felt to be stretching the club's constitution too far to admit one of the ancient enemy. Only the fact that there was not the remotest chance of making up the numbers without me (by which I mean not even a girlfriend in attendance) tipped the decision in my favour. Thus in one match in which the opposition were several short and we had to even up the numbers, I was the first to be given away. To my lasting regret, I made a second-ball duck.

of being dismissed by someone known to be permanently sozzled is very real. Such a fate befell Colm O'Donovan on the occasion of being bowled by Noddy. Noddy's place in NOBs history has been touched upon already, and it is a measure of what hard times we eventually fell on that he should ever have earned a spot in our Saturday afternoon side. On the occasion of this dismissal, more than one of his teammates asked Colm where he was going to drink in future, since it was obviously out of the question for him ever to show his face in Naughton's again.

This was, perhaps, a portent of an episode at a higher level some seasons back at the conclusion of a four-day Sheffield Shield game. Queensland had New South Wales by the throat on Saturday evening. It was obvious the game would end within ten minutes or so on Sunday. To encourage a crowd along, it was announced the two teams would play a one-day game following the conclusion of the Shield match. Queensland, with an appreciation of the spirit of such encounters,[2] decided to include someone from the crowd in its side, so a fourteen-year-old kid got to run around the Gabba with his heroes. More than that, he took two wickets, one of which was Steve Waugh, who, certainly not entering into the general festivity, was less than amused at the disgrace. Colm was certainly no Steve Waugh—but then it is quite impossible that a 14-year-old could be anything like so discombobulated as Noddy.

---

2   Until they finally won the Shield, there was always a touch of park cricket about the Banana-benders.

Most of our social matches were arranged on pitches either reasonably close to the pub or not far away, in the inner suburbs. For one of the NOBs vs Public Bar games we booked a ground in nearby Royal Park. Mats were laid and flags arranged, but no one had thought to bring bucket and spade, so we could make only perfunctory attempts at doing what was most obviously necessary to get the ground into a fit condition for play—that is, relocating somewhere outside the boundary line the monumental piles of horse dung scattered everywhere.

The game commenced with remnant heaps, and a judiciously weighted shot meant that you could probably run as many as six before the fieldsperson (this being a bisexual encounter) had tiptoed to the centre of the morass, tentatively kicked the ball clear, and rolled it around on the grass with the sole of the shoe long enough to venture a finger-and-thumb pick-up and twitch it in towards the pitch. Squeamish city types do not cope well with a bit of honest manure.

But the hazards of the dung heap were nothing compared to the wrath of the riders themselves and their entourage when they appeared, shortly after the start of play. The short, fat, pampered brats on runtish ponies that looked like they'd been sawn off at the knees we probably could have coped with easily enough. After all, they were only about ten years old and there were probably thirty or forty of us. More difficult of persuasion were the parents—fathers in moleskins and sporting leather patches on the elbows of tweed jackets to show how deeply they had entered into the dream of rural bliss, mothers perched imperiously in four-wheel-drives they had negotiated over rough terrain all the way from Ivanhoe and Kew. 'We ride here every Sunday!' they screamed.

Oscar Wilde in his day quailed before the fox-hunting fraternity of England, and there is something daunting about the equestrian breed and its total assurance of social and moral superiority, but on this occasion proletarian obduracy carried the day. We did have a full complement of six stumps, usefully pointed at one end, and a small array of bludgeoning bats with which to defend ourselves against the threat of a cavalry charge on miniature steeds, but there wasn't much we could have done against what seemed a possibility for a short time: a massed phalanx of Range Rovers tearing the surface off the oval. But in the end something must have persuaded them to give up the assertion of their prior right. It certainly wasn't our counter-claim that we'd paid the Council for the use of the ground. Perhaps it was their recognition of one fact that no observer could miss: once Noddy has put his Esky down, he's not going to move until it's empty.

The location of the ground so handy to the pub meant this game was notionally a home match for both sides—though in fact it was home only for those normally quartered in the stables—but sometimes in social games one side or other is on the road. If the team we were playing had travelled any great distance, our chances of success were enhanced by the fact that they would probably be half pissed by the time the game started, and totally pissed by lunch. Conversely, on the couple of occasions when we ventured far afield the quality of our cricket was somewhat variable.

Our two major expeditions both came about through the agency of Naughton's bar manager, our Club Patron Adrian Keeley. From his contacts in the trade he knew of another pub team who called themselves Tamleugh, which is an area just outside Violet Town, 100 miles north of Melbourne.

The usual arrangement of meeting at the pub and climbing into whatever cars were available was obviously not suited to a trip of this magnitude, nor were there likely to be enough (or indeed any) drivers in a condition to undertake the return journey. We would have to hire a bus and a driver capable of staying off the hops for the day.

The match was organised for a Sunday in March 1984—during the finals, which we were confident of not participating in. Having the Saturday spare, four of our number decided to catch the early train to Euroa, stay overnight, and be picked up as the bus went through next morning.

They chose to stay in Euroa rather than venture the extra ten miles or so to Violet Town, since they (mistakenly) believed there was only one pub in Violet Town. They counted on being thrown out at least once, and thought that Euroa's three pubs offered fall-back options.

When the bus came through Euroa at a very reasonable hour on the Sunday morning, Steve, Ian, Geoff and Colm were indeed waiting, slumped by the side of the highway. They were dressed for the game, but their whites were the only resemblance they bore to sportsmen. Their general demeanour showed all the marks of the previous day's indulgence.

They were relieved to be with us at all, because, they said, ten minutes before we got there the local cop car had cruised past them on the far side of the road, done a U-turn fifty yards on, and crawled back, pulling up beside them.

As the window wound down they thought of the various possibilities—indecent behaviour, consorting, vagrancy. The cop leaned across as they waited to hear the worst and said, 'I believe you boys won the quaddie yesterday.' As indeed they had. Modest though it was, they had made their mark on Euroa.

Though most were headed for ignominy in the afternoon, one at least was not to be entirely disgraced in the game that followed. The exception was not Ian Ewing, who, as captain, announced to us all at the drinks break that Tamleugh, 7 for 84 at that stage, were to be wrapped up as soon as possible. This produced a run spree for the home side, but the target they set was eventually reached (according to the annual report) thanks to a rearguard action by a most unlikely combination—Colm, Pat, Clem and (the oppo must have been totally boozed by this time in the afternoon) Noddy.

A couple of years later our Patron relocated, and became landlord of the Royal Hotel in Temora, New South Wales. To celebrate this translation, and to satisfy the curiosity of some of his new regulars—

hefty farm boys who fancied a crack at the city types—Adrian arranged a social game designed to test our resources to the extremity.

As a Wagga boy, I looked forward with relish to this encounter in a town only 60 miles from my old stamping ground. An innate understanding of the complexities of northern Riverina concrete would surely lend subtlety to both my batting and my bowling. Such depths of experience, however, did not come to my rescue, being more than counteracted by the predictable effects of such an opportunity for over-indulgence.

The formidable distance meant that this was not to be a one-day outing, but a long weekend on the road. A Friday evening start was decided on, with Beechworth being the first stage. One of the team party, our Number One Ticket Holder Frank Strahan, was part owner of the London Tavern, an old, delicensed pub there, which a syndicate was doing up to its former glory. There were plenty of rooms, some sufficiently down-at-heel even for us, so free accommodation for the troops.

The Hibernian Hotel just over the road was the focus of the evening's activities, during which one of us won the chook raffle. An unaccustomed triumph, it came at a time when no one was actually in a position to benefit from it.

There was a fall-back option, however. It had already been decided that, while the main group headed straight to Temora, one car containing the more respectable of my friends — in the circumstances a very dodgy choice to make—would detour into the city of Wagga and partake of a cup of tea with my aged and respectable parents. The chook would be an ideal token of friendship—overcoming even Baptists' prejudices against gambling.

After we set out from Beechworth it was clear there was a difficulty. The van carrying the bulk of the party naturally contained the large Esky with the ice and the cans—and, by an oversight, the chook. Emergency measures were required. A quick bit of overtaking on the double lines, lots of hand signals, and in the middle of the Hume Highway, in the centre of Albury, as the van drew in to the left and we came up on the open side, a brawny cricketer's arm extended from the van, carefully balancing the still half-frozen chook. A careful capture was effected from our port-side window (best catch of the weekend as it turned out), and the two vehicles took off to their chosen destinations. Just as well the Albury police were not as vigilant as their counterparts in Euroa.

I've never enquired of my parents how they enjoyed the chook, but the tea and biscuits certainly marked an interruption to the rest of the weekend's activities.

We stayed at Adrian's pub, with the expected consequence that the cricket was the least memorable aspect of the weekend. Saturday evening's pontoon game covered my expenses for the trip. Playing against a bunch of high spenders who had all lost the power of counting—let alone adding up to 21—made the job easy.

The most novel piece of social behaviour for the weekend was that at one stage Noddy fancied his chances of having it off with the waitress and was angrily trying to restrain some of the boorishness of other team members, whom he judged to be putting up his weights in the chatting-up line. For Noddy to find his colleagues a drunken embarrassment was an interesting new development.

When the game itself took place, NOBs were spared total humiliation by the fact that Temora was competing in the O'Farrell Cup that day, an event that took me back to my youth. It was the big game of the weekend in northern Riverina cricket—the town holding the cup being challenged in turn by teams representing the Associations from each of the surrounding towns. Temora were out to get the cup off Wagga, so the best of the Royal Hotel's cricketers were more seriously engaged (they might well have been trying to get the infant prodigy Michael Slater out), and anyone really interested in cricket had better things to do than play against us.

It was a straw in the wind when Stewie Mancer, who had played a season and more for NOBs when working in the kitchen at Naughton's and gone north with Adrian to warm the dim sims, decided to place his allegiance with his adopted locale. This was a double blow, as a couple of late defections had left us one short. Worse than that, Stewie could work up a head of pace that might be dangerous to batsmen in our condition.

No scorecard remains to memorialise the match, and no one who took part is willing (or perhaps able) to provide details of what happened on the field. A remnant photograph taken before the start of play gives a general indication of our state of preparaton. Only one stubby-in-hand is actually visible (Noddy's, oddly enough), but many more are etched into the faces of those depicted. The only question at issue was how early we'd be able to start the return trip.

Originally there had been some intention to make this an annual event. On departure, we all said, 'See you again soon,' but in truth few of us felt equal to a repeat performance, and it is unlikely that Adrian would have been quite so welcoming second time around. Not to mention the waitress.

Problems with the servant class were not confined to Temora, as the other great extracurricular activity of a cricket club is the team dinner. These were annual events, though in memory they all seem to blur into one monumentally sodden continuum.

Necessity made the club dinner a moveable feast, since no restaurant we chose to inflict ourselves on would ever have allowed us back. We went in for exotic cuisine—Turkish, Lebanese, Vietnamese, whatever nationality was newest on the scene and therefore ridiculously cheap.

Some of the younger members of the team, their palates accustomed to plain Australian fare, adulterated only by frequent visits to McDonald's, found the experience more than they could cope with. The night we went Greek, Steve Loney was heard to remark as the stuffed vine leaves were served, 'What the hell am I supposed to do with this—eat it or smoke it?'

By contrast, Noddy was never known to object to any choice of venue. Handcuffed to his Esky, it was a matter of complete indifference what kind of food, if any, was put in front of him.

The suspicions of the timid eaters were especially aroused on the occasion when we dined Turkish at a restaurant highly recommended by Club Patron Adrian Keeley. When it became obvious Adrian was not going to show up for the evening, Steve again commented, 'No wonder he's not coming—he's obviously been here before.'

This night was made memorable by the visit of Porky and Horse, Yorkshire mates of Mick the Snick, on holiday from the Old Dart. They had stopped off en route at Bali, where their northern pallor had been transfigured into lobster brightness, now flaking and peeling, exposing tender layers of blotchy skin. Late in the evening they delivered a particularly impassioned version of 'Yoong Albert got et by the lion' to the edification of the whole restaurant. Prior to this they had made themselves conspicuous when their mate Mick had made the first toilet visit of the evening. To mark the event, Porky and Horse produced party whistles which they blew at full volume, interspersed with cheering and singing. Every subsequent trip to the toilet by any of the company provoked another outbreak of festivity.

Notwithstanding such behaviour, the annual report unkindly suggests that the more socially disgraceful conduct for the evening came when I was entrusted with the duties of the Master of Ceremonies for the presentation of the annual awards, and proceeded to reorganise the restaurant. Most of the stories to be told and speeches to be made were undoubtedly of less interest to adjoining tables than to ours, so it seemed perfectly reasonable, not to say neighbourly, to get the couple dining at the table behind me to move to another table further away. A zealous MC needs room for manoeuvre, and the re-arrangement was clearly in the best interests of all parties.

Frank Hannigan's fiftieth birthday coincided with a possible date for an annual dinner, so we combined the two. We selected an elegant Chinese restaurant (a bit above our usual class) in the city. An angular staircase led to the upper level where we were ensconced; and like Briareos, the hundred-handed giant of ancient mythology, the waiter conjured a multitude of delicacies from the lower depths.

Towards the end of the evening, scores of dirty dishes, empty glasses and drunken diners lay scattered across the vast table. As the waiter began to clear things away he let it be known, to those of us sufficiently alive to sympathise with him for the work we had created, that he was especially proud of his carrying capacity. This led some irresponsible members of the team to urge him on to more heroic efforts—just another couple of plates, an extra rice steamer, the soy sauce bottle. He was like a camel laden for the Sahara.

Half way down the stairs the inevitable ensued. After the thunderous crash of crockery came the hysteric sounds of what we can only assume were Cantonese obscenities. The entire night's profits were swept out into the bin. This was another restaurant we chose not to re-visit.

The nominal purpose of the annual dinner was the presentation of the awards for the season just past. But because the presentation took place at the end of the evening, its ritual significance was always submerged beneath oceans of alcohol, not to mention the garrulousness of the M.C. Always as I launched into my performance, sighs of protest could be heard, 'Jimmo's off the long run again.'

The principal award was for the Most Valuable Player. This was undoubtedly a prize worth winning, since Adrian Keeley always donated a large bottle of top-shelf stuff for the winner. The triumph was somewhat diminished by the fact that tradition and the clamour of the rest of the company demanded that it be immediately opened. Once at least Steve Loney took home with him an empty Glenfiddich bottle. He did claim, however, to have drunk more of it than anyone else present, as was his right.

The other trophies, for batting and bowling, were of a more dubious nature. They were the handiwork (all on his own initiative) of one of our number, Dave McGaw, always referred to as Quick Draw. This nickname owed its origin to a comic strip character, but Dave's status as an art student gave it an additional resonance.

In the early eighties, few of us were familiar with the post-modernist movement, but when it came to destabilising expectations, Quick Draw was in the vanguard. Nothing further from the traditional engraved cup or silver-plated figure atop a bakelite base could be imagined. One must rely on memory here, because the trophies themselves have long since disappeared. They were in any case a species of performance art, so ephemerality was of the essence. Memory, however, insists that the bowling trophy consisted of an old cricket ball driven through by three or four six-inch nails, the whole encased in a lop-sided and rickety wooden box lined with red velvet.

The first reaction of anyone presented with one of these truly hideous items was to try to leave it behind in the restaurant, but no one ever got away so lightly. Quick Draw was always on hand, solicitous in pressing the offending item into the departing arms of an unwilling recipient. These creations became permanent trophies (that is, presented at least two years in a row) only because no one who won them ever wanted to keep them. Their disappearance was inevitable, though someone recollects having seen the batting trophy at the back of his garage six or eight years ago, but does not have the courage to actually go and look for it.

But by far the greatest disaster of all club dinners was a special one-off arranged in honour of Club Owner, Simon Byrne. Certain details of the dinner, held at a private club not a thousand miles from Naughton's, must be shrouded in anonymity to protect the reputations of those involved. Even so, only one of our number ended the evening in hospital, having laid his head open falling over in the ladies' lavatory. He had been forced to this desperate expedient by the fact that the gents' toilet was fully occupied by another of the company who had passed out completely, and at the end of the evening had to be manipulated into the back of a very small car and driven not to his home, since no one knew quite where that was, but to the driver's own home in Avondale Heights, on the opposite side of Melbourne. The host awoke at six in the morning to see his unwanted guest wandering around in the street outside, unsure quite which country he was in, let alone which suburb. It is not recorded whether his wife ever accepted the explanations offered.

Responsibility for the whole catastrophe was placed firmly on the array of imported beers the organiser had provided for pre-dinner drinks. The sheer alcoholic power of these exotic temptations has rightly earned them the nickname 'elephant beer', and on this occasion it proved the undoing of just about the whole gathering. Requests for civilised behaviour were warmly received and warmly responded to. The hapless organiser of the event was later summoned by the President of the club whose venue we had taken over. He prepared a contrite apology, excusing himself on the grounds that he did not know his guests were liable to such behaviour, only to find that he was himself the subject of investigation for telling the barman to perform an anatomically impossible feat.

Exactly how he explained this away we never found out, but as an epilogue it added zest whenever we regaled each other with the memory of an occasion altogether disgraceful to us, individually and collectively. Though somehow we never quite registered it that way.

The subsequent carpeting of our host added piquancy to a detail salvaged from the night itself. At the end of the evening, as we staggered through the vestibule into the sobering night air, someone still in the condition of being able to read observed that a notice of those standing for election to the committee of the club contained the name of the member who had organised our festivities. One of our number may have expressed apologies for having stuffed his chances so completely, but it was not sincerely shared by the majority, who found in it only additional cause for merriment. It was with considerable disappointment that we later learned that he had in fact defied the odds and got elected.

In any case, he was courting disaster by allowing his connection with a crowd like NOBs to impinge on social and professional relations of a more serious kind. In applying for jobs, promotions, or the dole, all NOBs carefully left blank the space that said, 'Community Organisations and Sporting Clubs'. Considering our behaviour *en masse*, it was something of a jolt to think that several members of the team occupied positions of dignity and standing in the wider world. It is to be hoped that the mention of certain names in these pages does not lead to a retrospective re-think on their suitability for offices of responsibility.

Though all this is long in the past, our mellowed way of life is only a superficial adaptation. Slowed reflexes, greater girth but diminished capacity, incipient arthritis and the gloom of mortgage have done their worst, but the spirit burns undimmed, because old park cricketers don't just fade away: they continue the struggle by other means. As previously recorded, Ian Ewing and Steve Loney took up lawn bowling when they forsook the cricket field—a commodious and affable sporting relaxation, one would think. On Steve's account, however, such appearances are deceptive. 'Lawn bowlers,' he says, 'are all ex-park cricketers. When it comes to sniping and scrapping and doing anything to put you off your game, they'll stop at nothing.'

It comes, therefore, as no surprise that Ian and Steve quickly found that lawn bowls was a game they were ideally suited to. Perhaps Pat O'Connor should consider re-establishing NOBs in a new format.

At least we wouldn't have to do battle with pony riders.

11

Trailing Clouds of Glory

The benefits to be derived from playing competitive sport are well known—health, fitness, team spirit, a sense of fair play, pride in one's achievements. The actual experience of playing for Naughton's Old Boys tended to undermine one's faith in these Olympian ideals— even before the Olympic organisers themselves provided such interesting examples of ideals in action.

If the physical exercise did us some good, we made sure it was immediately undone in the pub afterwards. As for the moral uplift, NOBs was an effective inoculation against such delusions. Being one of the NOBs was generally a chastening and humbling experience—not so much being thrashed on the field week in week out as the merciless detraction one suffered from one's team mates even— or especially—on the rare occasions when one had performed rather well.

In some other teams I played in—and in many opposition teams— it was instructive to see the sudden increase of cockiness in the modestly talented batsman who had been dropped twice on his way to 50 against paltry pie-throwers, but who now realised his true superiority to those around him. Equally tiresome were the long explanations of the donkey drop bowler who, if a wicket happened to fall his way through the gross negligence of an intemperate batsman, would take the whole of the interval whilst we awaited the new arrival explaining in detail how he'd been playing on the weakness he'd seen, drifting the ball away until he brought one back sharply to take middle stump, variations all so subtle as to have escaped the notice of wicketkeeper, slip, umpire—in fact, anyone in a position to see.

Absurd though it may be, it must be true that some of those who contest the game with passionate seriousness have genuinely convinced themselves that their performances are part of a gladiatorial contest of the highest importance, and their achievements a sign of rare talent. Every park cricket competition has its share of performers recognised by team mates and opponents alike as 'glory hunters'.

In the Northern and Combined there was a pair of brothers well known at our humble level whose abilities were sufficient to make them quite handy players in D Grade (which is another way of saying 'negligible'). Over many years they played in two or three premiership teams, and as a result of their efforts the club would be promoted to a higher grade. But there the club was left to flounder, as its two stalwarts would immediately desert, in search of another D Grade outfit they could boost to a Grand Final.

Lest it be thought they were totally mercenary in their approach to the game, it should be pointed out in their defence that they always turned up in another club bearing the proud descriptor 'Salvation Army'. Sister Anna may have carried the banner, but Brother Tom and Brother Fred were intent on carrying off as many flags as possible. Be it never so humble, there's no place like the top of the ladder.

It is difficult to enter into the thought processes of someone who has pitched his ambitions so low that a D Grade premiership in the Northern and Combined represents an achievement to be cherished.

No one who played for NOBs could delude himself into thinking that his triumphs were anything other than a more or less risible contribution to a rather pointless farce—and achieved anyway against an opposition no more talented than we were.

But it must be true that we could not have turned out game after game in sufficient numbers to put a team on the field (though that was often in doubt too) if some of us had not nursed in our bosoms secret thoughts that we were perhaps a class or two better than our detractors allowed—that had things panned out just a bit differently we could have performed with modest distinction at a level far higher than we found ourselves.

One of the drinking crowd experienced a similar sensation of a great career nipped in the bud during his footballing days. Leigh Astbury was not, strictly speaking, a NOB, since he never played for the club. But he did walk his dog round Prince's Park and if we were playing at home he'd stop for a chat and a laugh at our endeavours. On the day in question he was playing the match of his life for the Uni Blacks in the Amateurs competition, marking everything in sight and covering the entire opposing forward line. All this under the scrutiny of a Hawthorn talent scout who had actually come along to run his eye over one of Leigh's more fancied team mates. The object of the visit had a poor game and failed utterly to impress the scout. 'But,' he said to the coach, 'what about this bloke at centre half back?'

'Don't take any notice of that,' replied the coach. 'He's just having a day out.' And with that (undoubtedly correct) assessment died Leigh's dreams of a League career.

Just a very few NOBs didn't have to pretend quite so hard as the rest of us. Jimmy Wynd did indeed play with distinction at the elite level in football, and Steve Loney had played beside him in Grand Finals on the MCG. It is true that not all of the 100,000-odd crowd were in their seats for the Under 19s premiership, but there were some names of destiny going around out there.

During a period sometimes referred to as 'between jobs', Ian Ewing found his sole means of support was the $10 a week he got for playing for Northcote seconds in the VFA Second Division and coaching the under-16s, which led some to refer to him as a professional athlete. We were never privy to how much more he was raking in by way of endorsements. The contracts must have been huge.

Clem Simonetto was another whose sporting reputation was based more on football than cricket. Having grown to his full height of six foot four at a very tender age, Clem was first choice as ruckman for his school team. A year or two younger at St Joey's East Brunswick was a four foot nothing runt, who always seemed to have the football. Clem maintains, 'It didn't matter where I hit it, Ray Shaw would always get it.'

In time the same Ray Shaw played for and captained Collingwood, and though newspaper profiles of him never mentioned the debt, it was an article of faith amongst NOBs that he had learned all he knew about roving from Clem Simonetto. Some of us were moved to congratulate Clem on not having been a better teacher, since the balance just might have been tilted in the long and satisfying succession of Collingwood's Grand Final debacles in that era.

But when it came to cricketing prowess, merely playing for the NOBs was a public declaration that that door had definitely and finally slammed shut. As Peter Horsburgh, who had had the chance to know about such things, thoughtfully remarked late one Friday night training session, 'The trouble with NOBs is that it ruins you for real cricket.' And after another glance round the assembled motley he followed up with, 'I think there're a lot of blokes here playing with their last club.' As indeed there were.

Just occasionally, however, even at the depth at which we competed a performance will burst out of the mediocrity of our normal routine conveying the temporary illusion that something rather impressive has been achieved—a blinding catch perhaps, the equal of anything to be seen on the MCG. But with us it was not the expression of innate ability but an unrepeatable fluke, and likely to be the cause of much hilarity among one's team mates.

Inspired spells of bowling may occur in park cricket, but it is hard to tell when and if one is taking place, since batting collapses are so much the order of the day, and only moderate bowling is required to cause one. In fact the dice are loaded against really good bowlers, since the most awkward kind of delivery is unlikely to take the wicket of a batsman incapable of getting close enough to edge a ball moving away from the bat, and the matting surface so exaggerates the bounce that a genuinely hostile bowler usually clears stump height with ease.

The other aspect of the game where park cricket bursts forth in rare moments of glory is in spectacular displays of big hitting. When the eye is in and the bowlers have wilted for the day, suddenly all seems possible. And the park batsman enjoys a sense of triumph unknown at higher levels. It has never been recorded in the first class arena that a fieldsman patrolling the boundary has felt the need to shout a warning to the crowd that the ball is about to arrive explosively among them. On the grounds we played on it was a humanitarian duty to alert players on adjacent pitches, intent on their own pursuits, of impending danger. 'Watch out—ball coming' was a familiar cry, and the happy striker could lean on his blade, leaving to the humiliated fieldsmen the task of advertising his triumph.

I was once privileged to watch such an event from close quarters—about 20 yards away in fact. This was in my Sydney days, and Petersham Baptist were taking on St Alban's of Epping. A regular swathe was cut through our batting, and we went to tea eight down for just about 100. Having opened the batting, I was still standing forlornly at the bowler's end with 47 to my name. A wicket had fallen to hasten the tea break, so play resumed mid-over with a new batsman. Lloyd Jones would normally have batted about number 6 for us, but had been held up at work that morning and arrived at the ground barely in time to don the whites, the pads, the box and other necessaries in time for the resumption.

Lloyd was a firm-footed hitter, relying on eye rather than technique. First ball after tea he offered a short arm jab, well inside the ball, which bounced over the top of middle stump. Second delivery was a repeat performance. The dumpy and ageing off-spinner, confident of a second wicket in his long-protracted over, was clapping his hands and calling for the ball. He served up another, identical to the previous, and Lloyd played the same stroke, except this time he connected and the ball soared over mid on and the high paling fence into the school next door. They fetched the ball eventually, but Lloyd unsportingly put the next one back to the same spot. I settled down to watch and count as Lloyd laid about him. It was easy enough to keep a running score as almost every connection was either 6 or 4, with a slight preponderance in favour of the former.

Having given me 47 runs start, he beat me to 50. I later pretended that my two singles were just to give him the strike. From the ground we were playing on a large public clock was visible—on the old Peak Frean's building in Parramatta Road, for those who can remember what biscuits used to taste like in the 1960s. According to my distant reading of the clock, his fifty took ten minutes and his hundred a mere twenty. As I walked down the pitch to shake his hand he said to me, 'I'll try to give you a bit more of the strike so you can get your hundred.' A generous assumption—but by this time the bowlers were crying for their mothers. What really broke their hearts I think was when I managed to hit a six as well.

My hundred did indeed arrive, at which point our captain immediately closed the innings to let our fast bowlers loose on the spiritless opposition. Unfortunately he hadn't looked closely enough at the scorebook to notice that our unbroken partnership stood at 199 for the ninth wicket—still I would guess a record for the Sydney Churches' Competition. Lloyd had hit 14 sixes in his 140 odd, all done in 55 minutes. Each hit seemed to go further than the one before, and most of the time was spent foxing the ball.

The most unfortunate feature of this amazing performance was that the literal details so defy credulity that every time down the years I have tried to bask in the reflected glory of the event, my description has provoked only the bored scepticism of a public bar audience long inured to vainglorious exaggeration and downright lies.

One park cricketer of whom I was vaguely aware developed a simple but effective way of underlining his prowess to anyone who could be bothered listening to his report of the weekend's triumphs, which was to add a one on the front of whatever score he had happened to make. Thus even a first-ball duck could become 'ten or so' for the benefit of his workmates next week. And if he managed to make double figures, then his own sense of having achieved a landmark performance could be fully shared by his audience.

He was unfortunately brought undone by someone on the periphery of his acquaintance who actually played in the same competition and was in a position to check his account against the published record detailing the previous round's results usually issued by park cricket associations.

In any case, he should have learned what competitors at this level need to recognise; that there is nothing to be gained by boasting of one's performances in park cricket. As soon as the calibre of the opposition is taken into account all achievements are recognised for what they're really worth.

Nevertheless, once released into the outer of the MCG we grew in stature—the more so in the absence of independent observers capable of comparing our opinions with our abilities.

It was in fact at the MCG and equivalent grounds across the nation that we as park cricketers accomplished great deeds—the unacknowledged heroes of countless international encounters.

The games in which we actually took part could not possibly be said to have added to the glory of Australian cricket, so it follows that our supreme achievements occurred when we, personally, were not in a position to score a run or take a wicket. It was our advice, loudly and frequently given, that guided the actions of the more public performers who might have been lost without us turning the turnstiles and filling the bleachers behind them. The occasional testy hero who resented our astute assessments was clearly unaware of what we went through to swell his generous pay packet.

From time to time our deeply pondered conclusions rose even higher than the usual incisive 'Have a go, ya mug,' and we were able to feel that our contributions had turned the course of historic encounters. One such moment certainly occurred during the 1982–83 season, when a considerable gaggle of NOBs took the Friday off to attend the first day of the Victoria–New South Wales game, which was dominated by the batting of Steve Smith and Peter Toohey. In the longer term, neither quite lived up to his abundant promise, but on this day they were devastating. We had unanimously wanted to see the visitors bat, and McCosker out early did not disappoint us. His gritty efforts in Test matches had earned our approval, but we hadn't come to watch him today. First drop Trevor Chappell, who had achieved his moment of infamy on this ground two seasons before, looked both startled and annoyed at some raucous advice that he get out early so we could watch the batsmen, but obligingly complied with the suggestion.

One of the great tragedies of Australian cricket is that no one goes to watch the Sheffield Shield any more. Despite sometimes wonderful and attractive cricket, the crowd in a stadium built for 100,000 wouldn't keep even one chip seller busy. The fizz of an opening can[1] echoes through the concrete jungle of the stands and rolls out over the green sward. Every murmur is amplified by the mausoleum, so the players were fully conscious of any opinions we had to offer.

The Victorian team that day was a mob of kids—a young Dean Jones and a slim Merv Hughes still to make their mark. The score mounted dizzyingly as Smith and Toohey put the inexperienced attack to the sword. Yallop, Whatmore and Weiner all took a turn at the bowling crease.

Despite the massacre the young Vics never let up in the field. They ran their little hearts out and chased every shot right to the boundary. The exception was the senior player and skipper, Ray Bright, who stationed himself thirty or forty yards from the bat—always with someone in the outfield behind him to chase anything that got past. He had by this time long given up throwing in from the field—no

---

1   Obviously this reminiscence harks back to the time before we were humiliated by light beer served in plastic cups. What are reasonable precautions for 80,000 one-day hoons who go along to throw beach balls in the air and urge every female in sight to 'get yer gear off' seem a little unnecessary for the crowd of 250, only a small percentage of which might get drunk enough to overwhelm the two policemen present and stage a pitch invasion threatening public order.

disgrace in having a bung shoulder, but at a mere 28 years of age he really shouldn't have tossed in the sponge quite as conspicuously as he showed that day. It's still a bowler's job to try to get batsmen out, even on flat tracks. And some might argue that leadership is all the more important in circumstances such as the Vics found themselves in that day.

As his personal bowling figures progressed rapidly through the nineties for no wicket, we urged on his century with enthusiasm. The score stood close to 400 with three wickets down not long after tea, when the ball was played gently towards Ray in his deep gully position. For once the batsmen weren't running, so there was no pressure on him as he picked up the ball and bowled it back.

The keeper, Geoff Miles, in his first season for Victoria, had done as much as anyone to keep up the team's spirits in the midst of the awful flogging they were copping. Bright's wheeled return, from about 30 yards away, landed right at his toes, the most difficult spot to gather the ball. I offered the comment that it was the first time he'd hit a length all day.

At this point, frayed patience finally gave way and he turned towards where we were sitting, cupped his hands to his mouth and called out, 'Up yer bum.' Quite some time later, someone from an entirely separate group sitting a long way round the boundary from us also offered a less than kind assessment of the leader's performance. Once again Bright turned, but directly towards us, not the opinionated barracker, cupped hands as before and shouted, 'Up yer arse.'

Frequently it is said that, on top of all the playing skills, a captain these days needs to be an accomplished public speaker—though I think something slightly different from what we were treated to is intended by this. It is true that our comments throughout had been lacking in sympathy for the plight the Victorians found themselves in, and certainly having a barman with virtually nothing else to do for the day but keep us well supplied did little for our sense of decorum. We perhaps imagined our contributions to be rather wittier than they were, but they were a degree or two ahead of Ray's suggestion—and we had also paid for the right to deliver them.

It is nevertheless an unusual experience to find oneself barracked from the middle of the MCG by the captain of Victoria and we were fully conscious of the distinction conferred on us.

The mauling he and the rest of them suffered that day was not a unique experience in Ray Bright's career, but he was certainly well aware of a fact we older devotees on the other side of the fence had learned from much longer experience, that a day at the cricket is no picnic. Just ask the ex-girl friends who tried it! In the days before alcohol restrictions were imposed, a five-day Test Match was a gruelling experience that only the hardiest could see through to the end. One particular occasion recurs to mind, dating from about the time they started to turn off the tap.

Crowd behaviour was becoming a topic of comment in the press, and the ground authorities started to make noises about a perceived over-consumption of the amber fluid. With reason, too. I once saw a singleted warrior manhandling through the entrance gate a 44 gallon drum cut off at one end. Others of his party were carrying enough cans and ice to fill the drum. It seemed wise to choose a seat far removed from where this group facility set itself up.

But wherever one went in the MCG those days, there was a familiar sound heard once or twice a day, usually just before start of play. The cheapest kind of car fridge was a polystyrene number with a metal handle. Though of flimsy construction, it could contain a considerable weight of beer and ice. Age, exposure to sunlight, being sat upon by broad-bummed spectators, and general wear and tear would weaken the polystyrene to a point where a full load was more than the device could sustain. As the body of the Esky parted company from the handle the sound of cascading ice and bouncing cans (or—more dangerously—splintering stubbies) echoed through the outer,

accompanied by the cruel laughter of those of us already safely ensconced with a secure supply of chilled cans.

To combat the evils of alcohol during the forthcoming Boxing
Day Test some time in the late seventies, one of Australia's weirdest
press conferences took place. During it the then Secretary of the Melbourne Cricket Club, Ian Johnson, held up a strange contraption of a
size and shape no one had ever seen before and announced to the
assembled media that this was a 'standard-size' car fridge and that
nothing larger would be allowed into the ground. Even apart from
the fact that there was no restriction at all on how much more you
could buy inside the ground after you had exhausted what you had
carried in, it still seemed absurdly large to achieve the desired effect
of public sobriety. In justifying the decision, Johnson explained that
most people would want to include a certain quantity of ice as well,
but even without ice the Esky would hold only 18 cans of beer. 'On
18 cans of beer,' he memorably intoned, 'the average Australian will
become drunk but not objectionable.'

It was enough to make us inhabitants of the outer wonder just
what they get up to in the committee rooms of the Melbourne Cricket
Club.

The morning of the game there was a phone call from a mate,
Johnno, who expressed his concern about the new regulations. 'This
18 cans,' he said, 'is that compulsory?'

We decided anyway to brave the new order and arranged to meet
at the ground. Foolish youth (a category into which we half-fitted)
reacts to the imposition of limits with a bravado that can have coun-
ter-productive results. The first can was opened early in the day, with
a toast that was repeated with each successive fizz of the lifted tab,
'Drunk but not objectionable.' It was a long day and I have not the
faintest memory of who was playing let alone what happened, except that at stumps I was sufficiently aware of reality to refuse
Johnno's urging to accompany him to his usual watering hole. Next

day I made a late and bedraggled entry to the ground, and soon afterwards ran into one of Johnno's regular drinking mates who said to me, 'What did you do to Johnno yesterday?' I defended myself on the grounds that everything that had been done to him had been done by Johnno himself. Graham explained the question by saying, 'When he got to the pub last night he was quite objectionable.'

Overseas tours too could impose a severe burden. Several prominent players have commented on how wearing the constant schedule can be—but never have I seen one of them acknowledge what they imposed on dedicated supporters like us. A tour of England—five Test matches with play extending to 3 am down-under time—meant potentially 25 winter mornings when one wouldn't be much good for anything—though the English weather could be counted on for some respite.

An evening of quiet cans, then the telly at the foot of the bed was the standard regimen. And then waking in the reaches of the night to a blank screen, glancing at the bedside clock and muttering to oneself, 'Four for eighteen—those bastards never could bat,' before relapsing into befuddled slumber.

Just as video recorders allow today's soft youth to watch at leisure, without the feats of endurance we lived through in those dark dismal tours of the late seventies and mid-eighties, so too the video screen at the ground itself has removed all sense of risk such as we were accustomed to. Every sally to the bar for another half dozen cans or the quick dash to answer the consequent call of nature carried an extra edge of excitement—the knowledge that, however carefully you timed it, you knew you would miss the most dramatic moment of the day's play. As you stood in the queue or contemplated the porcelain the roar of the crowd would announce that a patient hour of sitting through soporific play had just gone unrewarded.

These days you can saunter back in your own good time and see it all re-enacted from six different angles.

This sense of deprivation was writ large during the Melbourne Test in the miserable Ashes series of 1978–79. Cricket was going through the trauma of Packer's World Series split, when the best players we had were otherwise engaged. The angst of long time lovers of the game was fully matched by the mania of the players themselves.

In all six Test matches, one or other of Australia's opening batsmen were run out, a collective folly of historic proportions. This exactly coincides with NOBs's original formation, and we modelled our game on the national team. Carefully programmed suicide at the top of the order was a distinctive element of our team strategy. Especially when Crossman and Radcliffe opened the batting together—neither of them exactly fleet of foot—it was often agreed between them that they would take a run off the first ball no matter what. It was surprising how seldom this resulted in disaster. With the non-striker taking off before the ball was bowled, it was very difficult to get a run out at the end he was headed for. Even when the ball dropped gently from the pad towards short leg three yards from the bat, the fieldsman casually bending to pick it up would often be so startled by the sound of grunting breath and galumphing boots, a few feet behind him and closing rapidly, that he would fumble the ball or hurl it to the wrong end.

But Gower and Randall in their prime were a shade above D Grade in the park, and enjoyed the easy pickings that resulted when XI of Australia adopted the same tactic. Devoted supporters all, we watched in gathering gloom the heavy defeats in Brisbane and Perth, before girding ourselves, with no hope whatsoever, for the Melbourne Test. The collapse of order in those dark days was obvious. For one thing, the Test didn't start until three days after the traditional Boxing Day hang-over cure.

An even 100 to Wood made the first day's play semi-respectable (Darling run out for 33!) but an early fold-up in the morning session of the second day left us nothing to discuss except the lunch menu. This is generally a highlight of the Melbourne Test. So soon after Christmas and collective bloatedness, it's usually possible to make a considerable raid on the family turkey and the leg of ham without anyone getting too upset. As we discussed the gastronomic future, an appalling thought arose to the surface of my mind.

I had decided to boil a few eggs to add to the feast, and nothing was more certain than that they were still on the stove. The prospect of the house burning down lent a degree of urgency to my move-ments. Brunton Avenue is the last place in Melbourne to try to hail a cab, but there was one breezing past right outside the ground. I piled in and got home to Fitzroy to find the gently simmering pot had only just boiled dry and no permanent harm was done to anything— except to a few terminally overcooked eggs. I was back in the cab and inside the 'G' in some sort of record time. With the break be-tween innings I had missed only three overs, but in that time Rodney Hogg, Australia's one hero of the summer, had smashed the top off the English batting, getting Boycott and Brearley for ducks and putting the Poms in a tailspin from which they never recovered.

Johnno informed me with great satisfaction that I'd just missed the most exciting moment we were likely to see all summer. And so it proved to be—our one victory for the series.

Sad to relate, even international careers as long and distinguished as ours are seldom given full recognition in the public bars and the footy pie nights when we feel our opinions could considerably elevate the level of discussion. We are forced to fall back on name-dropping, and, in the lengthening years since NOBs last rolled up their mats, we have all carefully embossed and polished any anecdotes that might allow us to boast of an inward acquaintance with the higher reaches of the game, chance incidents where we can claim to have laid a fingernail on the hem of glory.

That Mick Butera should be proud of his young nephew and godson—another Mick Butera—gaining selection as wicketkeeper for the Carlton Firsts is quite natural, and Mick would describe with avuncular approval the performances of his protégé. The better Mick junior performed (Victorian 2nd XI at the time of writing) the clearer it was from Mick senior's account that the art of the stumper was an inherited family ability. When the wonderful Pakistani leg spinner Abdul Qadir joined Carlton in 1998, Mick (who had never kept wicket in his life) was able to describe in more and more detail just how difficult it was standing up to the stumps to someone as devilish as the great Abdul.

The more often the score line 'st. Butera b. Qadir' appeared in the press, the greater waxed Mick's enthusiasm. There is no firm evidence he ever actually used the first person pronoun, but he seemed to become so familiar with the art of gloving a fizzing leg break that he had clearly made it his own. Someone not already clear about exactly who was who in these stories could easily have formed the misconception that Mick himself in his mature years was still regularly turning out for the Carlton First XI.

Another opportunity to join the immortals, in however honorary a capacity, fell to one of our number when he was visiting a celebrated curry house in the city. The Indian proprietor was well known for his passion for the great game, and, forsaking narrowly nationalist sympathies, he would assiduously woo to his premises all touring teams with a taste for strong spices.

However enthusiastic the visiting Pakistanis may have been for the flavours of home at the time they agreed to the outing, their mood on this occasion had been rather soured by events earlier in the day, the latest of a series of monumental beltings being handed out to them (and especially to the aforementioned Abdul Qadir) by Graham Yallop at the peak of his form.

Our informant suggests the players looked decidedly disgruntled on arrival, and their mood was not improved, late in the meal, by the host's sudden re-emergence from the kitchen regions, now bedecked in his finest turban and silver lamé Nehru jacket with a photographer in tow to memorialise the occasion. Their feeling of being rather used up for someone else's purposes was not assuaged by the obligatory signing of the bat they were asked to perform, and they left in sour haste very soon afterwards. The bat was left lying on the next table.

The temptation, Max says, was irresistible.

It is the usual fate of such trophies to find their way into auctions of sporting memorabilia, so some future auctioneer may well be faced with the task of explaining how it came about that the 1983 Pakistan team touring Australia included a player otherwise unknown to the pages of *Wisden* by the name of Max Radcliffe.

Max has not dared to show his face in the restaurant again, but is reliably informed that the bat, mounted in impressive style, is on public display, and the signature is plainly visible to anyone who examines closely enough.

Max's place in the cricket lore of the subcontinent does not rest on this performance alone, however. Some years beforehand, playing for the University Club XI, he had contributed a fluent 3 out of an opening partnership of 80 — but was not first out, thus showing that flashy starts are not the whole of the game. He had laboured to 22 when the fourth wicket fell, ushering in none other than the Nawab

of Pataudi, soon to be stripped of princely titles by his levelling government and therefore known to scorebooks on the Test grounds of
the world as Mansur Ali Khan. Off the last ball of the over Max was
run out—called through uphill and against a north wind, he claims—
having shared a partnership also of 22, though Max's personal tally
remained where it had been when the Nawab came to the crease. But
having batted with one of the legends of the game confers its own
small share of fame—and being able to blame him for running you
out increases one's stature immensely.

Acquaintance with the famous is apt to breed upon itself, as Pat
O'Connor discovered during a Test Match at the MCG. Sitting directly in front of him he thought he recognised an old NOBs team
mate, Fitzroy footballer Jimmy Wynd. Being a genuine sportsman,
Jimmy had not shared some of our usual characteristics — such as
length of time spent in the bar. There was thus not an entrenched
friendship to fall back on. Having pointed out the co-incidence to his
wife Pip, Pat was reluctant to force faded acquaintance upon his
chance neighbour. Pip, however, insisted he should at least say hello,
so Pat leaned forward and patted the supposed Jimmy on the shoulder: 'You probably don't remember me. Pat O'Connor.' The turning
figure extended his hand warmly saying, 'Good to see you. Wally
Masur.' At one blow Pat was thereby able to claim as bosom pals not
one but two Australian sporting icons.

Examination of newspaper photographs shows an extraordinary
similarity of feature between the two. So perhaps when Jimmy slid
off the list at Fitzroy and moved over to Adelaide to play, he was
frequently greeted in the streets as 'Wally' by those mistaking him
for the local Croweater hero.

My own claim to sporting immortality is not a small one, but it
is a still poorly known fact that both members of that formidable
opening pair, Mark Taylor and Michael Slater, trace their lineage (in
a cricket sense only) directly to me. This is not a frivolous boast

based on the fact, trivial in itself, that both come from the town where I grew up and learned my cricket. When Geoff Lawson graduated to the Test Team I took pleasure in the success of a fellow townsman, but laid no claim to having helped develop his outswinger or shown him how to bowl a bumper. But the case of Taylor and Slater is quite different.

When Michael Slater made a brilliant hundred at Lord's in only his second Test, I saw an interview with his father, filmed in his Wagga home, rightly proud of his son's achievement. There appeared to be an interloper perched on the end of the family sofa, but in time the camera swung onto the track-suited figure, and words appeared at the foot of the screen, 'Warren Smith, Michael Slater's coach.' 'Warren' he may be to a national television audience, but 'Bluey' he will always be to me!

The first time I ever made a real score—more than about 20— was at the old Bolton Park Number 4 Oval for West Wagga seconds against South Wagga in 1962, where I made 97 before I ran myself out. The innings included 27 off an over and the first three sixes I ever hit—two of them off my old mate Roger Craig. For most of this innings an even younger aspirant at the other end was compiling a more sedate 60 odd—none other than the left-handed Bluey Smith.

After I left town for the big smoke (and the small pond of Sydney Suburban Churches C Grade) I knew that Bluey had gone on to become one of the best cricketers in the local area. I was also well aware that Bluey had learned most of what he knew about batting from watching me from such close quarters that day at Bolton Park. Now I realised he had been not only watching and learning but subsequently passing it on to a younger generation.

Just a couple of years ago at a school reunion back in the home town, reminiscing, filling in a gap of thirty odd years, I mentioned to an old friend my claim to sporting fame. I was appalled to discover that he had been dining out for some years on pretty much the same story. He had lived next door to Bluey, and they played cricket in the back yard after school every day. And, he told me, before Michael Slater, Bluey had coached the young Mark Taylor, pointing out to me the similarity between Tubby's offside push and Bluey's own address to the ball.

At this point, I am ashamed to admit, I was forced to play the racial card. Who would believe, I pointed out to him, that Australia owed its two opening batsmen to a Serb named Drago Panič when there was a good Anglo boy like myself willing to claim the credit? Drago was compelled to recognise the persuasive force of my case.

Thus when I contemplate Taylor's 334 not out at Rawalpindi, or see Slater's slashing shot past extra cover off the back foot, I bask in the knowledge of where it all came from.[2]

Past one's peak and never having been anything like what one had dreamed of as a boy, the best one can fall back on is having been a 'formative influence'. This is a status Graham Baird has, from time to time, attempted to claim, since he and I went to watch his nephew Paul play in a school match somewhere out Wonga Park way.

Mentone Grammar had two star players, of whom Paul, captain of the side, was certainly one. Unfortunately, by the time we arrived Paul was already out but we did get to see their other good player belting the bowling all over the park. When 'Twisty', as he was known to his mates, finally got out we offered the comment, 'Well batted,

2   It is a matter for considerable regret that, when Mark Taylor recalls with affection several of his teachers at South Wagga Primary School in his autobiography *Time to Declare*, he does not include the name of my mother, who would certainly have been his teacher (though probably not his cricket coach) had not my parents moved to Newcastle three or four years before he attained the sixth grade.

son'—and you could tell the youngster was flattered by the compliment offered by two knowledgeable veterans of the game.

A couple of years later when 'Twisty' was well on his way to becoming a household name, Graham said to me, 'Do you remember watching Shane Warne play in that school match a few years ago?'

Recollection—until then dormant—was instant and total. Since we hadn't seen him bowl a single ball, not even roll his arm over to a teammate in a practice warm-up, it was hard to convince ourselves that we had given depth and subtlety to his bowling, but there was just enough there for us to be able to say, 'Picked him out as a schoolkid.'[3]

Certainly we had long prided ourselves on the astuteness of our judgement—like Johnno's instant recognition of the fact that Alan Border was too short to handle the bouncing ball and wouldn't last long at the top level.

There was a game we watched in concert where someone was snapped up rather nicely in the slips, and some of the company, with the enthusiasm that fills the veins some time after the luncheon adjournment, announced vehemently that it was the greatest slip catch ever taken.

Older and more experienced, I corrected them by naming what was in fact the greatest slip catch ever taken, and describing it in exhaustive detail. At the end of a long day, with no prospect of a tram heading in a Fitzroy direction, I decided on the taxi option and

---

3   Shane Warne is also the subject of my only successful cricketing prediction. As he was taking his couple of wickets an innings for Victoria and beginning to be mentioned as a possibility for higher honours his name came up in pub conversation. Having trundled the wrist spin at the lowest level and watched with particular interest many hopefuls come and go at Shield and Test level, I knew that if you're going to bowl leg breaks you must expect to get the tripe belted out of you every so often. In response to the observation that he was getting quite good figures, my assessment was, 'He'll never be a bowler until he's taken none for 150.' It wasn't long before Warne earned his first Test cap, and encountered Ravi Shastri on the best day of his career. Warne bowled well in patches with no luck, and duly took 1 wicket (Ravi Shastri's, in fact) for exactly 150. This was close enough for me to feel vindicated by his later performances.

wandered towards the nearest rank, outside the now extinct Southern Cross Hotel. As I paused at the lights at Exhibition Street I was
joined by a rather energetic gentleman, champing at the bit and anxious to get off the mark. When the lights changed he was off like a
startled rabbit, but to no avail. I arrived in leisurely fashion at the
vacant taxi rank, and there was my former companion, scanning the
horizon north and south. 'It's not often you can't find a cab here,' he
said to me.

It was a polite enough remark, but as a way of filling the brief
time we were forced to spend together it could not be compared to
my own conversational gambit, which was simply, 'Bobby
Simpson'—a fact he was unable to deny. As we shook hands I think
I said, 'You probably don't know me,' (I was right this far) 'but that
catch today they were calling the best ever wasn't a patch on the one
you took off Alan Davidson's bowling to get the Reverend David
Sheppard in the 62-3 series.'

Looking quite puzzled, he said to me, 'What—here in Melbourne?'

'No, no,' I said, 'the second innings in the Sydney Test.'

'Ah, yes,' he said with a smile of some satisfaction, 'that was rather
a good one.'

I was pleased to find that his recollection of events was almost on
a par with my own and graciously refrained from disputing the right
to take the next taxi then approaching.

The name of Graham Yallop, which has been mentioned a couple
of times above (he made 109 the day after Steve Smith's 200, but we
weren't there to cheer—and he was right in the middle of it when
Pat and I saw Australia's middle order of Hughes, Yallop and Border
contribute not a single run between them in the second innings at
Headingley in 1981) suggests a most unlikely association with NOBs.
When World Series Cricket split the game in 1977, the exodus of top
players left the Board team desperately short of experience. Bobby
Simpson, ten years retired, came back to captain the side in a re-

markable and entertaining series against India, but the Board gave him no guarantees for the England series the next summer, so when Brearley's team came here for the Ashes in 1978-79, Yallop, in his first Test against England, found himself captain.

Much comment was made on his lack of leadership experience. He had never captained Victoria—wasn't even captain of his club side, Richmond. The question was being canvassed on the ABC one day when one of the panel addressed a question to the expert comments man, who happened to be the old Typhoon, Frank Tyson: 'You were his coach at school, Frank. He must have been captain of Carey surely?'

'No,' said Tyson, 'we had a lad who was better than him.' The lad in question goes by the name of Graeme Mulvey, and it goes against the grain of everything that has been said in this book so far to reveal that the same Graeme Mulvey, through the accident of being a mate of Pat O'Connor, played two games for NOBs. In his first, in NOBs first season, he made 96 and so obviously showed himself way out of our class that he didn't play again for several years. His second game was not so productive, but still would have been enough to earn him the all-time career average trophy (if any such existed) were it not for the exquisite levelling process set out in the chapter on Ring-Ins. His name having got on our books early on, it stayed there and became a useful stand-by for a number of talentless recruits over the years, who dragged a lofty average down considerably.

But even discounting contributions by inept ring-ins, it must be admitted that Graeme Mulvey, whatever his schoolboy promise, failed to keep pace with his celebrated co-eval. Not that NOBs were entirely devoid of international expereience, however. Colm O'Donovan brought with him an authentic Dublin brogue and all the depth of expereience to be expected of one whose nation has always resented and despised English pursuits. A generous sprinkling of Yorkeshiremen, some courtesy of Pat O'Connor, others by pure chance, represented a sterner cricketing tradition. The West Indian infusion so hoped for by Pat[5] alas never materialised. Others of us within the team were able to bring to bear valuable expereience gained in overseas venues.

On my first visit to New Zealand I was dragooned by my host into playing for the Grace Road Gentlemen, an Auckland team whose name is redolent of Old World charm and the English village green— at least until one reflects on the fact that W.G. Grace was the most scurrilous and selfish hustler the game at the highest level has ever seen. He would have made an ideal park cricketer, in fact.[4]

The Grace Road Gentlemen were doing battle with a team known to me only as 'The Samoans', a bunch of strapping youths, all around twenty years old, except for one distinctly older and more dignified figure, appropriately captain of the side. It turned out he was a Methodist minister who saw the cricket team as his best means of keeping some at least of his flock from the lascivious temptations of the big city. If the post-match activties of the Samoans were anything like those of the Grace Road Gentlemen, this was a vain aspiration.

What the Samoans lacked in science they more than made up for in power. They could all (the Reverend included) hit with frightening velocity, but only to one sector of the ground. Anyone fielding closer than twenty yards from the bat was likely to have a hole drilled through him, but beyond that there should have been eight fieldsmen in the arc from straight hit to wide long on. The sole extra fieldsman

---

4   My own favourite Grace story concerns a game, common enough last century, where the county sides would play the posher public schools (two-day games—as long as a first-class match in those days) to instil in young minds the manly virtues of healthy competition. As captain (which meant he had to be a gentleman amateur even though he was paid five or six times more than any professional), Grace won the toss, whereupon W.G. and his brother E.M. opened the innings for Cloucestershire and proceeded to bat for the entire game. It is to be hoped that none of the young scholars nursed any further delusions about what constitutes a gentleman.

5   See page 62.

was needed at extra cover for the occasional mis-hit that ballooned out on the off side. Graham Baird, who lured me into this diversion, had a theory that they played this way because they came from islands shaped like teardrops and they didn't want to lose the ball.

Batting number 11 as the Gentlemen were skittled for not much more than 50, I was not able to make a definitive assessment of the bounce and pace of New Zealand concrete *vis-à-vis* the Melbourne variety, but I was proud that in keeping my wicket intact I upheld the reputation of Australian cricket amidst the craven collapse of Kiwi batsmen.

My second international appearance was a similar triumph at Spring Hall Green, playing for Halifax Police in the Yorkshire Gentlemens's Evening League. Sergeant Tim O'Connor, brother of Pat, clearly felt that the force needed some bolstering, or at the very least they should try to get eleven men on the ground. It was a strange but delightful expereience to start the game at about six o'clock and play on indefintely into the gloaming. I went in with eight wickets down and faced two or three balls (a nice back cut should have caught the eye of selectors for higher honours) before my support ran out.

Back in the Halifax Police Club, where I drank the cheapest beer I ever found in England and learned from the pie and mushy peas how fortunate we are to have broken the nexus with English cooking, Tim asked how I had enjoyed the game. I was pleased to be able to point out that, although my contribution was meagre, no Pommy bowler was good enough to get me out.

'Right,' said Tim. 'You're playing next week and opening the batting.' So a week later I returned to Halifax and Spring Hall Green and marched out at the top of the order. Somewhere in the second over, having kept my wicket intact for a ball or two, I answered what I took to be a loud call for a single. But the peculiarities of the West Riding accent made for difficulties in the lines of communication. Half-way down the pitch I realised my partner was standing stock still. Any slight problems the fielding side might have had were resolved by my slipping over as I turned, and I was run out by a considerable margin.

Disgraced and discomforted, I was not entirely humiliated, as I was still able to claim with perfect truth that, once again, no Pommy bowler was good enough to get me out.

I was pretty safe on this one, actually, and in his determination to take revenge for my boastful remark of a week before Tim had sold himself a dump because our opponents second time around arrived from Bradford and were Pakistani to a man. Whatever might befall me, I would still be one up on Pommy bowlers.

So with the Samoans in Auckland and the Pakistanis in Yorkshire it seems to me reasonable to claim a wide knowledge of the game in its international aspects. And yet you can sit next to these blokes at the cricket, some of whom might only have played District Firsts or Sheffield Shield, who nevertheless fail to defer to superior knowledge.

Well, back in the park we know the answer to that: 'Stick it up him, Slugger', 'Too good for this bludger', 'Let's have another', 'Knock his stumps over', 'Knock his bloody head off', 'Given 'em buggery'.

And of course, 'Talk it up, 'Towners, this ain't no turkey shoot!'

Stumps

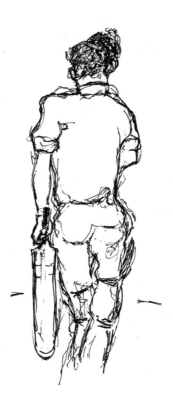

It's not always safe to revisit old haunts. A while back I found myself stranded, not far from the home ground of my first club in Melbourne. A tram had broken down somewhere, throwing the whole system into chaos. Too far to walk, not urgent enough for a taxi—best and most obvious option was to hole up in the nearest pub. Falling into conversation with a couple of regulars, I mentioned that this pub had been our local when I played just down the road all those years ago.

'I remember that mob,' said one of my new acquaintances. 'I played against you for Carnegie Church of Christ.' (So what was *he* doing in a pub? Well, he'd never known where the church was, but he always knew the closest pub — which is true to the spirit of Churches cricket.) 'You had a pretty good bowler,' he recalled, and he mentioned the Slug's name. 'He had me dropped caught behind twice, and then he bowled me.'

'Thanks for the memory,' I said. 'I was the keeper.'

Nevertheless, during the recent season around the start of play on a Saturday afternoon, I was wandering past a ground in Central Park, Malvern, where I'd played one game thirty years ago. I lingered to watch the new actors in the ancient rituals, as they relived our deeds of yesteryear.

I could vividly remember waiting with trepidation while the ominously named Randy Strongman ran in to bowl his riposte to my having whacked his totally undisguised slower ball over mid on for four. It turned out to be another slow ball, no less obvious, and I hit it to the same spot. But the bouncer was next, and he polished me off soon after.

A new generation had taken our places, but not a new dispensation. An hour or so of observing Eastern Suburban Churches C2 Grade brought back the authentic flavour of park cricket. One suspects that 'C2' was code for D, or even E—the level at which we began our climb. Well, not really a climb, more like toothpaste being forced upwards by a process of evacuation.

As I settled down to watch the game on my own former pitch I noted that the adjoining match was not only slow in starting but was soon abandoned altogether. A stroll in that direction revealed that the pitch there, rather than sitting slightly higher than the surrounding grass, was recessed an inch or so. It had rained heavily the night before. Some of the would-be participants—more enthusiasts than engineers—were bailing as hard as they could with assorted ice cream buckets and coffee cups. Twenty-two yards by two yards by even half an inch makes a volume of water that can't be shifted in cupfuls.

Abandoning that game meant picking up the boundary markers that had been already laid out—cute little plastic cones now, not the tatty flags we used to have—so an athletic young kid made a swooping run through the inner offside field of the game I was watching, startling various fieldsmen more intent on their own business, but perhaps clearing their path of potential dangers.

But the game I wanted to watch was the one on the pitch I'd played on.

They were better off for umpires than we had been at a much higher level—better off as far as numbers went, anyway, since one of the species was on duty. But he was obviously one of your law-of-averages umpires, operating on the belief that one appeal in three must be out. Which of the three was a mystery to the onlooker.

Square leg launched one solo but whole-hearted appeal for leg before—which the umpire turned down, but it must have counted in his calculations since the next hit on the pads was rifled out, even though the bowler scarcely bothered asking and no one else at all did.

It was the start of the game, so nerves were on edge and there was a good deal of chatter from both sides of the boundary line, exhorting teammates to higher efforts. 'Keep it up there — you've got him worried' meant that the bowler had hit the second mat after three long hops. 'Keep your head down—they'll come' suggested that, quite so early on, the almighty swing and miss was not the preferred option for the batting team.

A feature of the Northern and Combined competition was also the high level of discourse — or at any rate a lot of noise. 'Too good for him' from everyone behind the wicket as the ball flew past a flailing bat. I almost think I heard a ghostly voice crying 'Talk it up, 'Towners,' though no one ventured comparisons with turkey shoots.

Lush spring grass (no scruffy capeweed in the parks of leafy Malvern) and the recent heavy dump of rain meant that very few shots reached the boundary, and everything had to be chased. So the full range of athletic styles on offer in the lower reaches of park cricket was to be seen — the straight-backed high lifter of the knees, losing his cap in stride one and usually overrunning the ball by two paces; the tanglefoot flailer who seems in danger of breaking his elbow every time he throws the ball in; the fancy dan who's a tiger fielding off his own bowling but doesn't seem to think the other bowler's figures matter quite so much; the ageing boozer who long ago lost interest in that particular side of the game.

Even given such an array of fieldsmen, it was not surprising to see a total misunderstanding whereby an extrememly hesitant batsman of mature years managed to strand the impetuous young kid mid-pitch. Three catches went down, but not the one put up by the team slogger whose five ball stay saw one cow shot lob just wide of mid on before he put up a sitter for mid off. On his return to the team huddle he threw his bat ten yards towards the kit and loudly informed his mates, 'They're shockin' bowlers out there today,' as he ripped off his pads. His team-mates, though no doubt sorely tempted, circumspectly declined to venture an opinion on the quality of the batsmanship.

One was aware of occasions in the past when, crossing back to the passive side of the boundary line, one felt moved to disparage the quality of the attack. In the face of immediate and overpowering evidence to the contrary, there is a basic human need to convince somebody (who is of course yourself) that this is bowling you could take by the scruff of the neck and kick the living daylights out of.

This particular swaggerer was, like so many former colleagues and opponents, a batsman who needed to reach the boundary, as even in so short a stay he showed himself incapable of running two. Long hours of dedicated overtime in the bar were immediately visible in his physique.

One nice touch was the encouragement of the captain to a quite different breed of batsman: 'Well played, Peter — that was vintage you.' From which one inferred that this particular stylist had made the dead bat defensive prod his trademark shot.

It was pleasing to see the scorer miss one or two signals from the umpire for byes or no balls because he was too engrossed in the complexities of the form guide.

These were the authentic joys of park cricket, and all of NOBs was out there on display in one form or another.

No doubt, like us in our time, a hard core gathers on Boxing Day for the ritual outing to the G, where in the vast washes of the outer their skills are promoted as they never are of a normal Saturday afternoon. But never again will they follow our example of manhandling enormous Eskies filled to the gunwhales with beer and ice past compliant gatekeepers and through the sacred turnstiles.

Some of the best traditions of the game are gone, never to return.